Relaxation

Relaxation

JOSEPHINE L. RATHBONE, Ph.D.

LEA & FEBIGER  *Philadelphia · 1969*

SBN   8121-0266-5

Published in Great Britain by Henry C. Kimpton, London

Library of Congress Catalog Card Number: 70-85845

Printed in the United States of America

Preface

IN THIS CHAOTIC WORLD, with its widespread political and economic experimentation and uncertainty, the human element is threatened more than ever before. People have little sense of security. They are fretting because they are being thwarted, or they are over-exerting themselves in their desire to advance socially, financially or professionally. Furthermore, at the same time that the development and conservation of material resources are being stressed, very little attention is being given to the protection of human resources.

Human resources, however, are more essential for the welfare and perpetuation of any culture, particularly a democratic one, than are material or economic resources. No culture can survive and mature unless its men and women can be protected from threats to their physical-nervous-mental well-being, unless they can be permitted to obtain and maintain vigorous and abundant vitality, and unless they can be helped to recuperate quickly from stress and strain.

The stresses and strains of today play upon everyone. No one is immune to disturbing conditions in our culture and in our general "way-of-life." Some people, however, do not break down under the dangers to which all are exposed. Are they immune to disturbing factors in the environment and in their own lives, or do they know how to use resources for strength and calmness within themselves? They must have better psychological and physical health habits than others and know how to recuperate from strain through techniques in relaxation. Their healthful practices others can adopt, and their techniques in relaxation can be learned. This is our message.

It may take a great deal of perseverance for a person with poor health habits to refashion his life, and it will take determination as well as earnest application to learn new skills, but these requirements can be met. "Where there is a will, there is a way."

If it is possible to achieve physical-nervous-mental well-being, if there are means to obtain and maintain vigor and vitality, if one can learn to withstand stress and strain, the lessons must be learned in youth. The learning will be the most meaningful kind of *health education*; any physical or psychological techniques to be mastered will go beyond conventional *physical education;* any recuperative or restorative devices will bring about *re-creation*.

The methods of relaxing advocated in this book are both physical and psychological. It is as difficult to learn how to relax as it is for a person from the backwoods to learn how to drive an automobile. He has not seen many automobiles and has had no experience in avoiding them on the road. The tense person has had no experience with relaxation techniques, nor has he learned ways of avoiding frustrations and pressures. Both relaxation and driving take understanding, help and guidance, and persistent practice until new habits are established. Both require physical skill; and no skill becomes perfect without practice.

But one must not put the cart before the horse. While learning techniques for relaxing, one should discover the causes and first signs of tension. Only then can one be protected from the continuation or repetition of physical discomforts and of psychological manifestations of strain. While observing common signs of tension in other people—family, friends, and associates—one is helped to understand the causes for their complaints and frustrations. In this way one becomes, not only more understanding with others, but also more able to recognize danger signs in oneself, so that it becomes possible to get rid of causes of tension, or to control the effects before they become serious. This book approaches relaxation from both the psychological and the physical points of view.

Springfield, Massachusetts   JOSEPHINE L. RATHBONE

Contents

3. PHYSICAL FACTORS IN TENSION AND DISTRESS . 34

4. PSYCHOLOGICAL FACTORS CAUSING NEUROMUS-CULAR HYPERTENSION 58

1

Concern about Tension

THE FACTORS that lead to a full measure of health and potential energy are many, and when an individual has nervous instability, lacks calmness, or may be called tense, the sources of his condition may be difficult to find. They may lie in thwarting limitations of his environment, in handicaps which are his natural endowment, in disturbing emotional problems, or in personal hygienic indiscretions.

Even for the healthy and well-adjusted, environmental conditions today are extremely burdensome. The task of keeping poised and well is increasingly complex. Unfortunately, to the natural strains of living—the earning of bread, the winning of a mate, the rearing of a family, and the burden of growing old—have been added numerous artificial strains. The struggle for survival is more acute than ever before, and the environment threatens to submerge and defeat man.

Although societal and economic factors frequently are to blame for lack of vitality and inability to relax at will, a great deal of the responsibility for better health and less tension, even in times of social stress, rests on the individual himself. It is necessary for him to discover what factors should be modified in his own psycho-physical health picture, what balance of energy expenditure and rest will bring about his optimum or best achievements, what adjustments in his life patterns will minimize his worries, and what techniques will make it possible for him to relax. A man is of little use to himself or to society if his health is declining. He is of no real value if he is worn out by his work and dreads to begin his tasks each morning, if he becomes cross and impatient, if he is unable to relax.

Too few adult members of our society are satisfied with their accomplishments and way of life. They strive to get more and more done each day. Too many of them are unable to recuperate quickly from effort or store up vitality. They find it difficult to meet each day with enthusiasm and to keep their dispositions and faculties manageable until a reasonable retiring hour. Too many of them complain about such annoyances as insomnia, nervous indigestion, pain across the shoulders—all signs of tenseness.

The problem of how to achieve social and economic success and satisfaction and, at the same time, maintain vitality and composure is a very real one. It is possible that one could be better satisfied with his accomplishments and find an answer to basic health problems if he would study why and how he becomes tense, and what to do to counteract and offset fatigue. Fatigue and disturbing tension are not only the cardinal signs of ill health. They are also the direct causes of many malfunctionings within the mind and body, resulting in discomfort and ineffectual behavior. To find a complete explanation for what upsets health, comfort, and energy output, it is necessary to understand tension in relation to fatigue, to analyze the conditions as well as the hygienic indiscretions which commonly cause these manifestations, and to heed warnings about their consequences.

WISE PLANNING FOR HEALTH

One of the functions of education is helping individuals to plan wisely for health. Education can make clear that normal or temporary fatigue is wholesome, while abnormal or chronic fatigue is at the root of much discomfort and dysfunction. People can be taught to welcome a "good and tired" feeling as the reward for well-spent effort; but they should be taught, also, how to get rid of, not cover up, that feeling in order to prevent the disturbances that come eventually with accumulated and chronic fatigue.

This book aims to explain the physiologic as well as the psychologic causes of extreme fatigue and disturbing tension, and to describe how these causes may be counteracted or dispelled. It is written for tense people themselves as well as for teachers and others who may be given the responsibility of helping people to relax at will.

Those for whom the suggestions are made are described in the following chapters. They come from many walks of life, but they have certain qualities in common. They are enterprising. Some of them are students. Often they have such deep concentration on work, and so much eagerness to achieve that they disregard the vehicles through which their ends are accomplished—themselves. The expectation is that the majority of those who will find comfort and guidance from these pages will be conscientious toilers in the professions, harassed business men and women, hectic industrial managers, skilled workers in industry and dissatisfied housewives. Any individual who is carrying burdens and experiencing tensions for which he needs techniques in relaxation may find suggestions worth following.

It is sincerely to be hoped that no one reading these pages will think that simple measures, like more sleep or rhythmic exercise or studied discipline, are advocated when more drastic ones, like medicine or surgery, are indicated. It is the intention only to rally education to the assistance of medicine. Many physicians are eager that education find a way to help individuals to relax, for physicians know that such a non-medical measure has a great role to play in preventive or prophylatic medicine.

This book is concerned with relaxation as an aid in total fitness, not with other aspects of general hygiene. The emphasis is placed upon ways of offsetting and releasing tenseness, and not directly upon stamina and vitality. It is particularly timely to stress quiet of body and peace of mind as sources of strength, when so much is being asked of the human machine. Too few teachers and professional workers, and too few leaders in business and industry are sufficiently concerned about stability and serenity as means of offsetting psychophysical breakdowns and, indirectly, increasing stamina and vitality. The suggestions offered here are on how to prevent collapse of the psychophysical organism, not on how to drive it to its limits.

Psychological and physical aspects of ill health and tension are so closely interrelated that it is very difficult to decide which ones should be singled out first for attention. Who is to say, for example, that a man who has nervous indigestion should put the blame first on the fact that he is expending extra energy in his work, or that he has had a disagreement recently with his employer, or that he has been drinking too much coffee, or that he has been going without sufficient sleep? All these factors may be important, but he may have to reckon also with a poor physique. Perhaps his body can never stand the strains of vigorous, competitive living as well as he wishes. Perhaps he will always fatigue easily, and therefore must learn to conserve his energy and adopt every possible technique for adding an ounce of vitality to his meager store. Inevitably he may have to modify his urges and recognize that he cannot live as vigorous a life as he desires. For him, relaxation will mean doing less rather than doing something different. For another, relaxation may not mean doing less, but may mean rearranging his life and developing a new point-of-view. For someone else, it may mean only learning how to fall asleep at will.

CLARIFICATION OF TERMS

It is necessary to face squarely the relation of overstriving and overconcern to all types of overwork, overindulgence or overworry, fatigue and tension; and their relation to strain and stress. When the individual fails to adjust well to the demand of each day, he may be said to be under strain. No matter how heavy his work load or his mental and emotional burdens, if he reacts well and remains relaxed he cannot be said to be under serious strain. Nor will he show any stress. The individuals referred to most frequently in the current literature about stress are H. G. Wolff and H. Selye. The former has placed emphasis more upon the physical and especially the psychological causes of stress, and the latter refers to the physiological consequences of all traumas, infections and other attacks on the body by the term, stress. Only by paying attention to what both have said, is it possible to draw a full picture of stress.

According to Wolff, "Loss of sleep, exhaustion, pain, very loud noises, starvation, malnutrition, infection, sepsis and intoxication, by decreasing integrative capacity, make conflict relatively excessive. Likewise, acts that terrorize, humiliate, destroy self-esteem and create a conviction of being isolated, abandoned and unwanted may reduce integrative effectiveness."* Furthermore, the forced inactivity, which is so characteristic of the work situations of many high intellectuals and of their urban living conditions, may in itself produce profound effects, in the form of inability to relax and maintain health.

Selye is the one who has made clear the many physiological disasters which accompany such external influences. He has described a general adaptation syndrome (GAS) which manifests itself in adrenal stimulation, shrinkage of lymphatic organs, gastrointestinal ulcers, loss of body-weight, alterations in the chemical composition of the body, etc. The internal organs involved in general stress reactions, he states, are the brain, nerves, pituitary, thyroid, liver, kidneys and connective tissue cells, as well as the adrenals, white blood cells and digestive tract. If one wishes to be protected from the numerous disease states which stress can generate, he claims, one must be removed from a stressful environment or learn to relax.†

Wolff and Selye will make further contributions in Chapters 3 and 4. For the present they help to explain what will be meant at various times, in this book, by the word "stress." Before proceeding to a discussion of the nature of psychophysical hypertension and its psychophysical consequences, it is necessary to clarify many other terms which are frequently confused—normal fatigue, chronic fatigue, subjective fatigue, neurasthenia, mental fatigue, exhaustion, hypertonus, relaxation.

Normal fatigue is good. It is part of normal, healthful living. It may be recognized by a general tiredness of the body, not unpleasant in itself and dispelled by rest and sleep, and increased nourishment and fluid intake. Everyone who has known the joy of hard work has known the pleasure of normal fatigue. Those who are not afraid to work until they are normally fatigued, but who are willing to rest sufficiently to offset that fatigue, have experienced a rhythm of effort and release of effort, of physiologic work and physiologic rest which is wholesome and which never causes dangerous tension.

Chronic fatigue is pathologic, or abnormal fatigue. It often results from the disregard of normal fatigue and the necessary amount of

* Wolff, H. G. *Stress and Disease.* Springfield: Charles C Thomas, 1953.
† Selye, H. *The Stress of Life.* New York: McGraw-Hill Book Co., 1956.

rest to offset it, but it may result from other causes also. It may be due to deep-seated illness or to serious emotional derangement, and, in its turn, it may cause both physical and psychological illness. Chronic fatigue does not come suddenly, nor does it pass suddenly. It usually is a condition of long standing, manifesting itself in several ways: in persistent unpleasant feelings of fatigue, in actual decrease in physical endurance and mental achievement, as well as in the loss of zest for living and in lack of emotional balance.

Subjective fatigue is a term used to denote the individual's sensations or feelings of fatigue. The relationships between subjective and actual physiologic fatigue are somewhat confusing. Probably the difficulty lies in the variety of meanings attached to the word "fatigue." As indicated above, it may be used to describe a real physiologic state; or it may be used to denote a negative emotional appetite. "Fatigue," in the latter sense, is usually a sign of ennui or boredom, and affects work efficiency only as a deterrent on effort.

Some individuals have sensations of fatigue long before one would think they could be tired. Others seem never to know when they are desperately in need of rest. Both groups are actually ill—those who tire too easily as well as those who drive their bodies to extreme exertion. The first group exhibits lack of energy, the latter group exhibits lack of common sense. Whereas the individual who is constantly aware of his body may be abnormal, the individual who is never aware of his body is equally so. The latter is too likely to drive his body beyond its limits of endurance.

Many nervous, irritable, easily fatigued people will have heard themselves called "neurasthenic" by their physicians as well as their friends. Because this term is so carelessly used it is necessary to explain the several meanings which have been attached to it. Beard, who coined the term in 1869, used it to supersede the terms "nervous exhaustion" and "nervous asthenia," which were then used by the medical profession to describe the nervous elements in many diseases. He considered *neurasthenia* to be a want of strength in nerves, and treated it by constitutional tonics. Many other clinicians and writers since Beard's day have used "neurasthenia" as a synonym of exhaustion. They explain that usually the body adapts itself to meet the average requirements of its environment, but if the requirements become continuously maximal or if the organism is weakened by illness, by physical or moral shocks, then the neurasthenic symptoms appear. This explanation might be called the bio-neurogenic theory of neurasthenia.

Other physicians and psychologists have developed a different explanation for neurasthenia, which might be called the psychogenic theory. It is true that so-called neurasthenia has many psychologic manifestations. Feelings of fatigue often are the cause of an individual's refusal to perform a task which would be accomplished without any neurasthenic symptoms if it were found to be satisfying. According to this view, neurasthenic individuals have an obsession of fatigue which distorts the entire picture. Psychologists who support this theory say that neurasthenic fatigue is felt particularly in actions which are induced by will, while actions prompted by desire are only slightly influenced by it, at least as long as the desire is strong enough. In this sense, neurasthenia does not consist of a decrease of nervous strength but a convulsive increase of strength and an inclination to over-effort. The proponents of this theory emphasize that neurasthenia is not a phenomenon of degeneration, and that we have more cause to consider it as increased but misdirected vitality. In other words, according to this view, neurasthenia may be either a device to avoid work or an early sign of real fatigue—fatigue in its stage of "neuromuscular hypertension." If one is tempted to call himself or someone else "neurasthenic," he should look for typical signs of physical exhaustion (bioneurogenic), but at the same time seek possible psychologic reasons for the avoidance of work by simulating symptoms of fatigue (psychogenic).

Many people are troubled with so-called *mental fatigue*, even when they disregard sensations of bodily fatigue. Mental fatigue is the term to designate a slackening in work commonly called mental or intellectual. The physiologic or bio-neurogenic factors causing "mental fatigue" are of the same nature as those causing fatigue in general. The psychologic, or psychogenic factors are more prominent in "mental fatigue," and tend to overshadow the physiologic factors. Mental overwork is serious, not because it involves the mind in contrast to the body, and not only because it appears in those intellectuals upon who society should place much responsibility.

2

Mental overwork is serious because it leads so rapidly to neuromuscular hypertension—the forerunner of exhaustion and breakdown.

In physiologic terms, if fatigue be carried far enough, it results in complete cessation of work. This is the state of *exhaustion* in which there is little possibility of restoration of energy through will power, increased nourishment, rest and sleep. Exhaustion is the final stage of fatigue, when the breaking down processes exceed the building up processes, and the organism is forced to stop functioning. True exhaustion means collapse. The human organism rarely reaches such a state without dire consequences. When the early signs of fatigue are neglected, however, exhaustion is a consequence to be feared.

Strain and *tension* precede fatigue. Strain is something done to a person; tensing is something he does. Tension is good when it leads to action; but mounting tension, either physical or mental, without action, becomes stress in the conventional use of that word. Selye would emphasize that it causes the generalized adaptation syndrome (GAS). Tension, long-continued, is the problem in our modern culture which has called for this book.

In studying physiologic and psychologic fatigue, one discovers that a phase of increased neuromuscular tension appears in all forms of excessive activity. Since the medical profession has chosen to use the word "hypertension" to describe a state of the heart and arterial system, it is less confusing to use the term *hypertonus* in describing general or localized excess muscular tension (*tonus*—muscle tissue in a normal state of activity or vigor; *hyper*—too much).

It is unfortunate that it is necessary to use such an unusual word as hypertonus to explain the actual and primary condition which has to be dealt with in counteracting excessive tension. It is fortunate, on the other hand, that the condition is so specific and so easy to treat. Too much (hyper) tension in the muscles (tonus), although it may be persistent after effort has passed (residual), can be relieved quite easily if it is recognized and if proper techniques are used. Residual hypertonus may develop in any muscles of the body—in the arms, legs, trunk, or viscera. It is not necessarily to be considered as something pathologic. It is just a condition attendant upon overuse of muscles, particularly upon holding parts of the body still in postures necessitated by work, especially when movements that would normally release these postures are arrested. It is something to be counteracted to insure comfort and efficiency. Wherever it arises it can be attacked. Only when it persists too long can it be called a pathologic condition.

Hypertonus in the neuromuscular system always precedes exhaustion. If it is counteracted, exhaustion will not develop. People who live normally and wisely live rhythmically, and alternate periods of effort with periods of release from effort so regularly that fatigue is temporary and leads neither to hypertonus nor to exhaustion. They never need to study techniques for releasing tension, because their normal manner of living excludes the building up of excessive tensions. For most people, however, life is so demanding that neuromuscular hypertension or hypertonus is common, if not continuous, in some part of the body.

Obviously, then, hypertension in the muscular system, or hypertonus, is the stage in fatigue which should interest the clinician and layman. It is important to discover exactly what hypertonus is, how it exhibits itself, and how it may be offset. One should learn to recognize various signs of excess tension in the nervous and muscular systems, and to bring relief by the expedient of *relaxation*.

Within the human body, during life, muscles are never fully relaxed. Just as they never become completely exhausted, they never become completely relaxed. In a medical dictionary, the definition given for relaxation is: "Diminution of tension; languor." In Webster's dictionary "to relax" in the transitive form means: "To slacken; make less close; render less tense, rigorous, or severe; divert, as the mind; loosen, as the bowels; make languid," and in the intransitive form, "To take relaxation; become less severe or close." The limiting state of hypertonus would be extreme contraction. Normal living is a state intermediate between these two extremes.

THE "WHY" AND THE "HOW" OF RELAXING

If a person were inclined to spend too much time in relaxation, it would be important to introduce into his life a little struggle and concern in order to make it more normal and well rounded. Most people in our society, however, are not spending too much time in relaxation. They are living in an age which is abnormally exhilarating. They are living with fear. Some of them are striving incessantly for more of this world's goods, or for more satisfaction to the ego, or for more success in social relationships. Others are engaged in selfless activities without expectation of personal gain. All are constantly "on the go" and are trying to find clues to how to relax at will. They are dissatisfied with the "warp and woof" of the loom of life, and they want to weave a new fabric. The introduction of some threads of relaxation into that fabric will make it both more durable and more beautiful.

Techniques of relaxation are numerous. Some of them attack the health habits of those who need to modify their patterns of living. Some of them attack directly the hypertonus in muscles. Some of them soothe nerves. Some of them reduce the strivings which keep people tense. Some of them substitute worth-while activities and philosophic concepts for the petty schemes which drive individuals to hectic over-effort. All these means of offsetting and counteracting extreme fatigue and tension constitute the "How" of relaxing. In the following pages, this "How" will be explained. So, also, will the "Why."

ROLES OF MEDICINE AND EDUCATION IN RELEASE FROM TENSION

In order to help people to relax, a great many techniques are being used. They are being advocated by many specialists within the professions of medicine and education—by physicians, physical therapists, psychiatrists, psychologists, recreation therapists, and physical educators especially.

Most patients enter their doctor's presence, on the first visit at least, in a state of tension. They are uncomfortable; they are worried about themselves; or both. They are frowning, their jaws are clamped shut or their teeth are grinding, their shoulder girdles are raised, their elbows are flexed and their hands are clenched. All this the physician notices before the patient sits down. Then the patient does not settle back comfortably but remains perched at the front of the chair eager to recite his complaints. No wonder that the first drug the physician prescribes is a relaxant.

As he listens to the patient on his first visit, the physician is very attentive to the descriptions of the pains which have brought the patient to him. They are the warning signals which the physician has been trained to interpret. The physician has specific drugs and surgery with which he can deal with the causes of the pains, provided they are real and not overlaid with too much anxiety. It is natural that there should be a component of anxiety with any pain, so the physician has to be concerned with his patient's anxiety as well as with his pain.

There is a movement within medicine to reduce the quantity of drugs prescribed for many ailments. A little magazine called *The Sciences*, published by The New York Academy of Sciences has carried articles recently on the medical use of *Sleep Therapy*, as well as on the dangers of *Deprivation of Sleep*. Investigators have looked at the ways sleep can be induced to treat disease, to improve chances for survival and recovery, and to relieve anxiety in a variety of severe physical and psychological illnesses. It has been stated that eventually sleep research may provide enough knowledge about the body's and the brain's save-and-repair abilities to lead medicine to a vastly overhauled system of therapy. (See Chapter 7.)

Some of the new methods of inducing sleep involve use of electricity. Needless to say, physicians will not discontinue the use of narcotizing drugs kept under their control, or the good old stand-bys of physical therapy—heat and massage.

Although a person falls into sleep most readily in a cool environment, nothing is more soothing for body discomforts, which can be disturbing sleep, than heat and gentle massage to part of the surface of the body. Heat can be given in the form of heating pads or by salves which serve as counterirritants to draw blood to the surface of the body to make it feel warm, or by hot baths or by electric modalities. Massage, in its turn, is the very kindest way to give tender loving care (TLC). In states of sensory shock from emotional or physical injury, massage gives a comforting awareness of the body surface. Following a sedative massage to the back or head, a patient often states that the painful area of the body, wherever that may be, seems less dominant. Without doubt, proper massage lessens sensitivity to the body's surface and gives a sense of well-being which reduces, if it does not eliminate, pain. Pain is one of the chief causes of tension—both physical and psychological.

When uncontrollable tension keeps recurring, physicians will refer patients to the specialists within their ranks who specialize in mental disorders—the psychiatrists. They are the ones whose patients are deeply distressed, whether causes are grave or inconsequential. Many of the patients seem to be bottled up inside; have personal relationships in a tangle; have an overpowering sense of isolation; and be in a state of reflex fight or flight; with a quickening of heart and breathing rate and obvious neuromuscular hypertension. These patients have obsessional traits; are neat, methodical, precise and feel a particular need of always being in control of a situation. Most of them are highly intelligent and sensitive. The psychiatrists must change their stress (in the Selye sense) to ease.

Psychiatrists have subtle ways of giving their patients catharsis as well as supportive therapy. Some of them are direct in their suggestive therapy: others use all manner of devices to divert the minds of their patients into less threatening channels. Some of them use hypnotherapy, a combination of limited insight therapy combined with hypnotic suggestion. All of them have been more than appreciative of time worn techniques of counselling, religion and recreation. They have all tried to help their patients achieve wholesome love relationships.

Within educational circles, during the past half century, a professional group known as psychologists has developed. They are concerned with the relation of man to his environment as well as to himself. They have developed the theme that disorders of mind and body are the reflections of a disorganized society operating on a susceptible individual. One of the techniques which they have used most effectively is group counselling. To be sure, it is a technique used also by psychiatrists, and with very great skill. The difference between how psychologists and psychiatrists use this technique, is in the depth of the probing. After observing many therapy sessions conducted by skilled technicians from both professional groups, the author can state that the psychologists operate best on the level of common sense, and that patients for whom deepest insight is needed and for whom that insight may be traumatic should be under the care of a psychiatrist. The object of both psychiatrists and psychologists is that patients shall gain self-control. Those who have been psychologically ill must grow to understand themselves and learn to operate without leaning on any one else. Actually, the efforts of any other persons in their treatment are not important: the patients themselves must achieve the desired results.

If a group of psychiatrists were to be asked what other educators had had beneficial influences on disturbed and tense individuals of all ages, they would undoubtedly single out recreation therapists* and physical educators. Psychosomatic medicine is predicated on the thesis that anything which can be done to help a person physically should help him psychologically; or, rather, that he is ill psychophysically and should be reached at any point in the syndrome of his pathologic condition. Anything which can be done physically to relieve or to quiet a person who is in an excited state may encourage a sense of peace. Anything which will enliven a person who is depressed physically and mentally may make him happier. Any medium which may be offered a person to express his troubled thoughts may give him relief. Any chance he can have to gain approval may make him feel better. Any satisfactory social relationship may reduce his egocentricity or his sense of aloneness, and lessen his symptoms while his basic difficulty is being uncovered. On all these tenets, recreation can have a share in the rehabilitation of a psychopathic patient.

A recreation leader, as well as every other adjunctive therapist, however, should understand his limitations in treatment. The recreation specialist has his particular role to play, and it is a very important role indeed; but he must never think that he, alone, can bring about a cure or even a remission of symptoms. He can only help the patient, with other members of a rehabilitation team. Direct treatment of physical symptoms will be left almost entirely to physicians, nurses and physical therapists. The recreation worker

* Rathbone, Josephine L. and Carol Lucas: *Recreation in Total Rehabilitation*, Springfield: Charles C Thomas, 1959.

will be expected to treat psychological symptoms mainly. What has been said in regard to psychopathic patients can be said just as positively about tense and troubled people who cannot be said to be "sick," but are just unable to relax at will.

The recreation worker will have been trained very often with physical educators. These two groups of professional workers are educators, essentially, rather than therapists. They should be able to discern an individual, in any group, who is in need of techniques in relaxation; should be able to help him learn how to balance his strivings and egocentricity with untensing activities and sociable escapes. They must be examples of what they preach and try to demonstrate. Recreation specialists and physical educators cannot be effective with tense individuals unless one can trust them and depend upon them. They must be friendly and "outgoing"; strong physically and therefore towers of strength; calm and resourceful because they are confident of their abilities. Perhaps their goals in life have not been very high economically, but what they have aimed at they have reached, and other people sense their satisfaction with life. If a recreation specialist or physical educator does not exhibit these traits, he will not be able to help an insecure, fearful, or distraught individual who needs to learn how to relax. This book is essentially aimed at helping people to find repose and peace of mind through methods which are more educational than medical.

2

Signs of Tension and Strain

ONE SHOULD RECOGNIZE THE SIGNS as well as the causes of excess tension before investigating techniques for its release. There may be overlapping between signs and causes, and, in some instances, signs will reveal causes. By dividing the discussion under these two headings, however, there is less danger of neglecting factors which may be of particular interest to the individual who is himself troubled with inability to relax or to the reader or therapist who is concerned about the problems of others with whom he comes in contact.

Outward signs of neuromuscular tension are varied and less obvious than the person in need of help supposes. They may be grouped under appearance, findings of physcial examinations, and annoyances of which the tense person or his associates complain. All tense people do not exhibit the same signs. Some will suffer from rather minute and specific physical irritations. Others will be chronic complainers of this and that ache or pain, while some will be more distracted psychologically than physically. Still others will not complain of anything, but will be sources of anxiety to their friends and physicians because they do not take care of themselves, and will be unwelcomed members of most groups because they are so excitable and erratic.

APPEARANCE

Tense people are not slovenly and careless in *appearance*. They usually are well groomed, spritely in bearing, and often exceedingly

15

acceptable socially. Many tense people have cause to be proud of social position or previous attainments. They have been busy, and worthily so. Although they may have done those things which they ought not to have done, they have never left undone those things which they ought to have done. These are among the reasons why "there is no health in them."

Tense people are not flabby. A characteristic of individuals exhibiting persistent hypertonus is the firm, rounded, and well-defined configuration of the muscles in contrast to the indefinite contours and untensed quality of the resting muscles of the ideal athlete, or of the aesthete. Although the tense person's muscles may be shapely, they are not resilient. This non-resiliency or inelasticity of tense muscles exhibits itself particularly when one is in motion. It may not be as easy for an unskilled observer to recognize a tense person by his movements as by his held positions, but physicians and students of human nature learn a great deal about a person from watching his movements. These movements are actually more revealing to a keen observer than what the complainer says about himself. When a person moves gracefully and freely, anyone should be able to see that he is well, both physically and psychologically. When he is restricted in his movements it is a clear indication that he is not relaxed.

MANNERISMS

If you were to ask your neighbor what are the most common mannerisms of a person with tension, he would list fidgeting, twitching, trembling, biting nails, wringing hands, cracking knuckles, tapping with fingers, twisting a handkerchief, etc. Many tense people do show signs of extra motility, but they also show signs of rigidity and arrested movement. They often hold parts of their bodies very still and cramped. Perhaps it is their heads which they hold to one side. Perhaps they hunch their shoulders. Perhaps they twist their legs around chair legs when they sit near a desk or a table, or cross their thighs always in one direction. These held positions are quite significant in light of an understanding of physiologic fatigue. Motility is usually a device for counteracting or upsetting muscular tension. Blinking of the eyes, twitching of the mouth, and grimacing apparently act as relief mechanisms for a state of mental tension, with its accompanying muscular hypertonus; while tapping with the fingers, beating time with the feet, or wriggling in a chair afford changes of position, better circulation, and thus less tension. Movements may suggest the state which is popularly called "nervous," but that state is not always synonymous with the state of hypertonus.

Many tense people do not appear "nervous." On the contrary they often appear very calm. Actually, they are restrained. Unfortunately, many individuals who are in serious need of relaxation try to keep themselves immobile because they fear that they will reveal "nervousness" by movement. They do not realize that they are increasing their tensions by holding themselves still. The only positions in which a person can be still and truly relaxed are leaning against a support or lying down. Of course, some people do not even relax when they lie down.

POSTURES

Numerous students of industrial fatigue as well as physicians and teachers of physical education warn against what they call poor *posture*. The type of posture which they describe as the result of fatigue, and also as the cause of fatigue, approximates the senile stoop due to weak muscles. It is the posture of exhaustion—that final stage of physiologic fatigue. This posture, however, is not as tiring as one in which the muscles are trying to hold the weights of the body against gravity. That is the reason fatigued people assume it.

When we see a young woman slumping so that her lower abdomen is thrust forward, we may be quite sure that she is not strong enough or rested enough to hold her abdominal wall retracted. When we see a young man with his head in front of his chest and his back and neck markedly curved, we may be sure that he is temporarily or chronically lacking in health and vitality. He is not tense; he is weak muscled. On the other hand, when we see a young person with head erect, neck straight, chest nicely balanced above a retracted abdomen, and weight poised forward, we may be quite sure that that person is neuromuscularly alert and active. But any person may tire himself unduly if that attitude becomes strained.

The danger, as far as muscular tension is concerned, is not so much in slumping of the body segments, as in holding of the segments in whatever positions are assumed. The latter element in all postures is, neuromuscularly, the more costly of the two. The human skeleton is so loosely articulated that every active posture necessitates considerable, if unconscious, muscular effort. Every posture becomes fatiguing eventually, the aesthetically and mechanically "good" as well as the ungainly and inefficient. In fact, so-called "good" postures are often more taxing to the neuromuscular system than so-called "poor" ones. The average so-called "poor" posture permits the skeleton to hang on its ligaments; the so-called "good" posture necessitates the balancing of skeletal weights by the action of antagonistic muscles.

Although strain is always placed on muscles when units of body weight are held against gravity, no one type of standing or sitting posture is peculiar to tense individuals. While many of them stand erectly and carry themselves beautifully, others are awkward in bearing. The truth is that all standing and sitting postures demand tonic contraction of muscles, and, if any held position is maintained long enough, the involved muscles become hypertense, give real discomfort, and cannot readily be relaxed at will. Postures, long maintained, are all causes of residual tonus in muscles. Holding any position for a period of time will make one tense and uncomfortable.

HEIGHT-WEIGHT RELATIONSHIPS

Whenever persons with residual neuromuscular tonus are studied in respect to *height-weight relationships*, no clear-cut type is revealed. Apparently, neither excessive slimness nor excessive stockiness is an absolute indication of residual tension or excitability. Some slender people are tense, and some stocky people are tense.

Possibly the explanation for excessive tension or its opposite, in relation to body build and weight, must come from the doctors who know how to appraise the glands of internal secretion. Many students of the body, as well as of the emotions, are hopeful that continuing research in the field of endocrinology will lead to a better understanding of neuromuscular reactions. It is easy to understand that when internal secretions are modified the whole body may react to the modifications. It is hazardous, however, at least for the time being, to accept as a definite causal factor those secretions concerning which very little is actually known. Instead of accepting the hypothesis that the glands are the controlling agents for neuromuscular activity, we may come to know, eventually, that glandular activity and neuromuscular activity are both results of common factors. When conditions are found together, it does not mean that one is the cause of the other. Both may be signs of something else.

It must be acknowledged that underweight and overweight are usually the consequence of undereating or overeating. The reason that height-weight relationships cannot be accepted as indications of individuals' inability to relax is because tension and stress operate variously on the eating patterns of tense individuals. Some people lose their appetites when they are tense, while others become ravenous. Some people are so worried and fretful that they do not think of eating, while others escape into gluttony just to think of something pleasant instead of something which is worrisome. In one instance they will lose weight; in the other they will gain. Some people waste away from undereating, while others actually gorge themselves to death, all because of worries and in spite of medical help.

During routine examinations, doctors and teachers of health and physical education often recognize definite symptoms of excessive tonus which the individual has not associated with tension and stress. The physician, of course, is not only interested in the tension in muscles, resulting from their holding of the skeleton in various postures against gravity, but he is also concerned with the effects of skeletal and visceral slumping upon joint structures and upon internal organs.

RESTRICTION IN JOINT FLEXIBILITY

Almost without exception tense individuals do not move with freedom and grace. In the early stages, this lack of freedom in movement may be due solely to lack of flexibility and inability of muscles to relax sufficiently to make possible full range of movement. The part of the skeleton that becomes most limited in mobility when an individual is tense is the spine. Those individuals with persistent tension throughout the body and discomfort in the internal organs are the ones with the greatest limitation in mobility of the spine. One must be cautious about assigning either to a flexible spine or to a healthy internal organ an explanation for the associated factor; but it is well known that these conditions are closely related.

RESTRICTIONS IN BREATHING

Associated with limitation in flexibility of the spine and with discomfort in internal organs is limitation in flexibility of the chest resulting in restrictions in breathing. Have you ever heard a person sigh deeply after a bout of strenuous effort, or after an emotional shock? Have you ever figured out why that sigh occurred? The diaphragm and auxiliary muscles of breathing had held themselves partially contracted during the emergency, not relaxing for some time, and then had gone into powerful contraction followed by maximum relaxation. The sigh was the relaxation phase. Imagine how disadvantageous to the total body as well as to the internal organs are long periods of restricted breathing due to over-effort or to anxiety.

Signs of excess tension in the respiratory system are choking attacks, asthma, laryngospasm, spasmodic coughing, and irregular breathing. Many tense individuals suffer acutely in the breathing mechanism. One who had this complaint was a young druggist. His breathing was quite irregular and he told of having severe choking attacks. He had not had a real vacation for years. He was scrimping on sleep because his work made it impossible for him to get into bed until one or two o'clock each morning, and he was rising early three mornings a week to attend university classes. When he was long past the age of usual undergraduate work, he was trying to collect points for a Bachelor's degree, as a means of changing his profession. For several years, since an exhausting illness, he had experienced distressing emotional reactions against being alone or turning a corner. Besides the choking at night, of which he complained, he was found to have extreme residual tension in the muscles of breathing, in the right arm, and in the region of the pelvis and hip joints. His muscles were of good shape and firm. His sensation of muscular tension was very poor, at first, and during observation his breathing was shallow and irregular until some degree of relaxation could be established. It was conscious relief of neuromuscular hypertonus rather than any medicine which eventually brought about a reduction in his symptoms. He began to breathe more freely after he had learned to relax.

A woman teacher had frequent asthmatic attacks. When she was in bed she had to be propped up on three pillows. Doctors were watching her heart because of essential hypertension. One of them asked a physical educator to teach her some relaxing techniques, particularly for the diaphragm. She was found not to be able to take in a deep breath, but particularly not to be able to expel air efficiently. The range of motion of her chest during breathing was very little, indeed. After practicing techniques suggested in Chapter 5 and after acknowledging what had caused her to be tense, her blood pressure went down and her asthmatic attacks disappeared. The doctor, who had referred her to the physical educator, kept her under observation and slight sedation, mainly to be ready to counsel her if the anger which had caused her stress were to recur.

POOR CIRCULATION

It is astonishing how many tense people have disturbances in the circulation. Some are troubled with excessive flushing of the skin, some with excessive perspiration, and a great many with cold limbs. Everyone recognizes the blushing and perspiring that accompany occasional attacks of "nervousness" and fright. Everyone also associates a flushed face and neck with more continuous states of tension accompanying acute disturbances in the functioning of the heart. Many laymen, and even physicians, however, fail to recognize the relationship of slight chronic tension to disturbances in the capillaries and in the heat-regulating mechanism of the skin. Yet these reactions are satisfactory gauges of hypertension, both neuromuscular and arterial.

A very frequent circulatory accompaniment of residual neuromuscular hypertension is blanching and chilling of the body surface. Many tense individuals complain repeatedly of this symptom. Some claim to be cold most of the time. Others are always pale. Physiologists have performed many experiments which show that the pallor associated occasionally with ordinary exercise is due not to rhythmic exercise but to static contraction as the result of held positions, or to anxiety and excitement.

A case in point is a young woman whose paling and chilling was in the hands and arms. She was carrying great responsibility and doing most exacting desk work in an insurance firm. She attended a corrective physical education clinic only when her symptoms became unbearable, and she usually admitted being in the midst of preparing an address or getting a department report into shape. It was after writing or engaging in mental effort, which would eventually be recorded in writing, that her hands and arms appeared most tense and chilled.

A young man complained of discomfort definitely in the feet and lower legs. His arches showed signs of static strain; he had been given arch-supports with only mild relief of symptoms. Massage and rhythmic exercises always made the feet and legs feel much better for several hours after treatment, but, until his general tenseness was treated, his symptoms in the legs always returned the day after the treatment. They were never apparent when he was walking, but became acute after he had sat still for two or three hours. His associates claimed that he was exceptionally alert, was always on the edge of his chair eager to participate in discussion, while he gripped his legs around the chair legs. It was at such times that he complained of his legs becoming numb with cold, tingling, and feeling prickly. It was surmised that another reason why this man got the overdose of tension in his legs was because one of his daily occupations demanded considerable static contraction in the act of standing on the alert. He was a court attorney.

It is to be observed that the young people whose histories of tension have been reviewed briefly have all been from business and the professions—a druggist, a teacher, a writer and executive, and a lawyer. They represent those who need techniques in relaxation most—they and skilled workers in industry. Anyone who is familiar with "laborers" in these categories can bring to mind many more case histories revealing excessive tension. Think of the many doctors who wear themselves out solving the problems of others while they neglect themselves. Think of the horde of school teachers of both sexes who are driven to physical and psychological breakdowns in stimulating immature personalities and neglecting their own. Think of the many young women in the profession of motherhood who become distracted and acquire personal complaints because of irritations and overwork. Think of the many recruits to skilled labor and industrial management who break down because they are not protected from unnecessary occupational strain.

One factor in many instances, of course, may be lack of perfect health, antedating the added burden of overwork and worry, and the excess fatigue and tension. For example, some discomforts for individuals with residual neuromuscular hypertension may be due to the fact that they are anemic. Beard, many years ago, observed this possible connection. He stated that anemia might accompany the state which he called neurasthenia. More recently, pernicious anemia has been recognized as accompanying neural and psychic symptoms, and exhibiting itself by numbness, tingling, and weakness. From the Peter Bent Brigham Hospital in Boston, where hundreds of cases of pernicious anemia have been studied since the institution of liver therapy in the summer of 1925, it has been reported that many show neurological changes. The early signs are often girdle pain (abdominal), backache, neuritis (brachial and sciatic), and mental changes.

Certain other blood changes have been recognized in cases of increased nervous excitability. The white cell count of man is known to be very unstable. When it is high, the individual is usually considered unwell. During rest in the recumbent position with complete physical and mental relaxation the leukocyte (white blood cell) count is steadiest and at a minimum. It changes as much as 60 to 100 per cent with variations in activity, such as moderate exercise, changes in posture, and even changes in the mental state. The minimum of leukocyte count is to be found during the period when an individual's condition approximates most nearly complete physiologic repose, and tends to rise with any increase in his mental and physical activity.

This increase in the count of the white cells may be due either to an increase in their production or to their redistribution. The number of both red and white cells in the circulating blood under varying circumstances raises questions relative to the function of rhythmic exercise in liberating these cells from their storage places, as well as to the effect of posture on congestion in the abdominal area. Also, the increased tension of the heart and vasomotor system generally, as an aftermath of increased tonic contraction of skeletal muscles, raises questions relative to the effect upon the heart itself of general neuromuscular hypertension.

DISTURBANCES IN THE DIGESTIVE SYSTEM

Action of the diaphragm affects the digestive system also. Lying as it does just above the stomach, its up and down motion mildly massages the abdominal organs. A very common accompaniment of generalized hypertonus, with restricted flexibility of the spine and chest, is dysfunction of the liver, stomach, and colon. As everyone knows, when a person has any exhausting experience, is subjected to any pleasurable or unpleasurable excitement or any undue mental or physical exertion, he may have an accompanying gastrointestinal derangement. Motor or muscular disturbances of the gastrointestinal system are exhibited often in constipation and diarrhea. The circular muscle fibers of the colon, which are normally more sensitive than the rest of the tract, may become so irritable and tonic that they cramp down and interfere with the progress of food and its residues. Or, when the irritability becomes extreme, the muscle fibers may cause diarrhea. Both constipation and diarrhea can result either from "nervousness" or from the tension of extreme fatigue alone.

Many tense subjects complain incessantly of constipation. Two cases are chosen for special discussion since they reveal particular aspects of the larger subject of residual neuromuscular hypertension.

One young woman's day was full of petty irritations and constant activity in the static sitting position of the overworked secretary and typist. For months her evening meal had afforded no relish and had "lain undigested for hours," according to her own report. Her physician had recommended corrective physical education, under strict supervision. Her condition improved slowly under a regimen of conscious relaxation and graduated rhythmic exercises to a satisfactory conclusion. For the last month of exercises, the young woman complained of no indigestion. Her job was as difficult as previously, but she had learned how to relax.

Another woman claimed to have been constipated "all her life." She had a low, protruding abdomen. The treatment for this case in the corrective gymnasium did not consist of strenuous exercises for the abdominal wall, but of passive and active exercises to increase the flexibility of the chest cage and to reduce the "spasticity" of the diaphragm, as well as the tension in the muscles of the shoulder girdle, arms, and legs. Apparently it was reflex tension of the sphincter muscles in certain regions of the gastrointestinal tract, associated with hypertonus elsewhere, that had caused her constipation. This explanation seems sound in light of the fact that her "symptoms" became much less disturbing as her neuromuscular tension decreased under treatment.

Many persons troubled with hyperactivity of the muscular wall of the colon call their condition "colitis," and even submit to colonic irrigation without satisfying results. Others call their attacks "chronic appendicitis," but, although they are under expert medical attention, appendectomies are not always suggested, and the condition gradually subsides if they can be taught to relax.

With most muscular reactions of the gastrointestinal tract, sensory symptoms are also present. This fact raises the question of the relations between irritability in the smooth muscle of the internal organs and increased reflex tension in the skeletal muscles. It has proved difficult to decide how much an acute gastrointestinal upset of dietary origin, for instance, might increase the tonus of the general neuromuscular system. If acute pain is present, it is quite possible that there will be a tendency for the muscles of respiration and the flexor muscles of the trunk, at least, to be affected. If the subject is emotionally concerned about his gastrointestinal sensations, there may be an increase in general hyperexcitability from that source. It appears, however, that sensory impulses from the gastrointestinal tract do not increase reflex tonus of the skeletal muscles as frequently as tension of the general musculature, from whatever cause, call forth gastrointestinal symptoms, such as colic and "heartburn."

Secretory changes in the gastrointestinal system often accompany sensory changes. Scientists have suggested that as fatigue toxins circulate through the body they may affect the digestive gland cells, and that the secretion of digestive juices is less active after muscular fatigue. Emotions definitely affect the digestive secretions. Some observers claim that decrease in gastric acidity is greatest when the muscular exertion is accompanied by emotional excitement, and so suggest tranquillity of mind, as well as rest of body for a short time before and after a meal, in order to augment gastric acidity. It is important to realize that the normal secretions of the stomach wall are acid reacting, all advertizing regarding the dangers of "acidosis" to the contrary.

It seems foolish to dump lemon juice into the stomach to increase its acidity, or bicarbonate of soda to counteract the regurgitation of the natural acid because of antiperistalsis due to hyperactivity of the stomach wall, when a good rest and a dose of facing reality and taking oneself less seriously would set matters right. Some observers claim that different emotions have different effects on the digestive fluids, and suggest that secretion can be induced by pleasurable emotions and stopped by unpleasant or painful ones. Restaurateurs who offer sweet music and soft lights with banquets are therapists as well as good business man; and housewives and hostesses who set attractive tables and keep their families and guests in amiable repartee are physicians of body and soul.

HYPERACTIVITY OF OTHER ORGANS

During emotional states, as well as during strenuous physical exertion, other organs of the body seem to be affected also. For example, it is common observation that one is forced to urinate frequently during strenuous mental work or when under emotional strain. It seems altogether feasible to conjecture that, in human subjects, mental or emotional stimuli which bring about reflex postural patterning of the skeletal muscles may cause, also, reflex tonic contraction of the "smooth" sphincter muscle of the bladder, thus necessitating frequent urinating. It would be interesting, however, to measure the quantity of fluid given off under varying conditions and to determine whether the bladder is constricted in volume or the entire urinary system functions more actively during states of increased neuromuscular tonus.

Another organ that may become seriously tense as well as congested is the uterus. Apparently hypertonus of the skeletal muscles causes a reflex hypertonus of the smooth muscle of the uterus in the same manner as it affects the other hollow viscera. The most common cause of serious dysmenorrhea, or pain at the menstrual period, is the "colicky" uterus with hypertense cervix. Cases of menstrual congestion as the result of inactivity and sagging abdominal muscles with suspected "weak" uterus can be relieved comparatively easily. Those cases associated with hypertense skeletal muscles generally, but especially in the pelvic and abdominal regions, are difficult to treat.

These observations afford evidence that individuals with residual hypertonus in their skeletal muscles have also various hypertensions in their smooth (visceral) muscles. No one type of smooth muscle seems to be affected. To summarize, the trachea, esophagus, blood vessels, stomach, intestines, bladder, and uterus all give evidence of increased spasm. Hypertension of the skeletal muscles from whatever cause will result in a reflex hypertension of the muscles of the hollow viscera and tubes. Why one individual has malfunctioning in one organ while another individual has different complaints is not clear.

PAIN AS A SYMPTOM OF MUSCULAR TENSENESS

Pain in these organs or elsewhere in the body may be a symptom of muscular hypertonus. In skeletal and smooth muscles, the more intense and sustained the hypertonus, the greater the discomfort, and vice versa. Everything increasing tonus in hollow viscera or in gross muscles tends to cause pain. If a device can be found to decrease tonus, pain will be decreased. Relief of pain is an indication of decrease in hypertonus and its many consequences.

Physiologically, these two enemies of comfort—pain and excess muscle tension—are almost synonymous. Why, then, is a person not always suffering acutely when he is tense? Because, psychologically, the "threshold" for perceiving pain varies under different conditions. A "threshold," in this sense, is a psychological barrier to physical perception. It is like a wall between two chambers. In chamber one is a fluid which will spill over into chamber two, but is held back by the wall, or threshold. The fluid is the stimulus to physical pain. When it gets into chamber two, it is perceived. The wall is what holds it back. This wall, or threshold, changes in height under varying conditions, of which one's degree of alertness versus fatigue is the most direct as well as the most subtle.

Excitement and psychological stimulation raise the threshold, and discomfort is not perceived readily. Boredom and psychological depression lower the threshold, and even slight degrees of hypertonus are perceived as acutely painful. Everyone must have experienced this swing in threshold. Who has not "forgotton" a headache or a stomach-ache when a situation has become really interesting? Do not men and women who immerse themselves in the hectic and exciting world of affairs forget the aches and pains that distress them at home? Much discomfort can be explained on the basis of changes in threshold of pain perception with lessening of excitement or loss of contentment.

It is quite apparent, then, that psychological factors contribute causes of excess muscular tension. Some of the signs of tension are also more psychological than physical, or appear to be a combination of the two. Although physical symptoms of hypertensive fatigue are bad enough in themselves, they become even more trying when combined with psychological disturbances. Then they annoy one's relatives and associates as well as oneself, and lead to criticism and strained social relationships. Nobody likes a tense person, particularly if he gets irritable and distraught.

IRRITABILITY TO ENVIRONMENTAL FACTORS

Just as one becomes more sensitive to pain as fatigue increases, so one becomes more aware of noises and other environmental factors. There is no doubt that intense noise is very generally disliked, and that when for any reason a person becomes irritable and fatigued, noises become more disturbing. In order to shut out, as it were, the effects of noise during acts demanding concentration, the tendency is for the body musculature to become hypertense in attitudes of attention. In order to concentrate in a noisy environment one must work harder. That is the explanation for some of the fatigue which is experienced in city offices, in industrial shops, and in ordinary schoolrooms.

Tense people also become sensitive to the behavior of other people. We say that they become "touchy." Words which are spoken in jest or "by way of comment," are taken seriously and personally. Friendships become ragged, quarrels grow in magnitude, family and business relationships become strained—and all because one or both individuals who should be seeking an agreement become tense and irritable.

EFFORTS ON THE PART OF INDUSTRY TO RELIEVE STRAIN

The results of hypertonus may show in one's work as well as in one's personal relationships. In industrial plants efficiency is greatly reduced by fatigue in its stage of hypertension. The consequences are spoiled work, time lost because of discomfort and illness, and accidents. A case in point is a young man who, as soon as he graduated from a liberal arts college, took a position in the drafting room of a large factory working on war production. Since he had had some experience in stage designing and commercial drawing, it seemed appropriate for him to serve his country in the emergency by using these talents. Unfortunately, he was not physically fit. His muscles were not conditioned to hold his body in the position necessitated at the drafting board. After a few weeks of fatiguing hours, with his trunk leaning forward without support for long periods, the specific muscles which had to hold him against gravity went into contracture or cramp. The sensation must have been like the pain at the base of the skull and in the nape of the neck, experienced by typists and piano players and writers; but it was very acute. It involved muscles lower down on the back and ones which are associated with deep breathing and lateral movements of the trunk. He was in agony and could not continue at work until he had been treated with heat and massage. Before he had given up, his work had suffered and he had become very irritable. If he had been working at a lathe instead of at a drafting board, he might have had a serious accident because of the disorganization of his movements following the spasm and pain.

The non-industrial worker might well study his own case in the same light. Why should he not recognize that his headaches and irritating indispositions may be due to fatigue? Why should he not blame his errors in judgment, his miscalculations, and his periods of irritability with subordinates and associates on tension and overwork? They are the forms that "spoiled work and accidents" take for him.

DISREGARD OF FATIGUE BY MENTAL WORKERS

It is muscular work that fatigues, to be sure, but who can say there is no muscular work during mental endeavor? The muscular activity associated with mental work is definitely of the tonic type, exhibiting itself in poses of attention and arrested movement. The increases in tonus with states of attention are quite widespread in the body, with some individual variations. Very common manifestations, however, are the slight but definite forward posturing of the head, the restrictions in volume of breathing because of increased tonus of the diaphragm and other muscles of respiration, and "setting" of the muscles of the shoulder girdle, lower back, buttocks, and legs to raise or hold the body alert.

The first sign or symptom of overuse of these muscles during mental work is discomfort. Many mental workers complain of pain at the nape of the neck, across the shoulders, in the lower part of the back and in the legs. They need to rest their bodies periodically as do manual or industrial workers, and release these tensions occasionally by rhythmic exercise. If they do this, they will not have the more serious consequences of too much mental work—intellectual deterioration and emotional breakdown. In fact, their mental work will never become "too much," if they will guard the body from residual muscular tension. The brain does not fatigue, nor does it become tense. Only through disturbed movements of the body does distraction or disorganization of the mind reveal itself.

OVERACTIVITY

It is interesting to note that a person who is overfatigued and tense is likely to persist in overwork or hyperactivity. Whether this reaction is to be described as physical or psychological is hard to decide. Probably it should be termed "psychophysical." As indicated above, toward the beginning of the hypertensive stage of fatigue one becomes more alert and active. In this stage, one also drives the body and intellect on hectically with no thought of consequences. When one is too tired, as during experiments with deprivation of sleep, or when one must go without sleep because of an emergency, one seems to lose all sense of proportion and to welcome a breakdown as eagerly as a holiday.

Usual overactivity, because of lack of wise planning, takes two particularly dangerous forms. One is overaddiction to business, the other is immersion in a social whirligig. Overaddition to business is particularly vicious because there is an element of virtue associated with work. In the United States, especially, a very high evaluation has been placed on work. Even when work has killed men and broken up happy homes, it has been praised.

Immersion in hectic forms of recreation is even more deplorable than immersion in business. Unfortunately, many forms of commercial amusement are overstimulating and useless. Furthermore, few people who are tense have sense enough to select forms of recreation which are relaxing. Few of them have taken the time to learn the benefits that can come from unexciting diversions, such as reading in one's own room, making useful things with one's own hands, and enjoying the out-of-doors, preferably with one's friends.

The most deplorable aspect of the activity picture of the overtense individual is that he does not know how to prepare for recuperative rest. He thinks that he can keep desperately active for sixteen or eighteen hours a day, and then slip off into limitless sleep for the remaining eight or six. If he finds, to his dismay, that sleep does not come readily when he jumps into bed after a thoroughly exacting or exciting day, he is quite confused. He does not realize that the wheels of the mind and the levers and guy-ropes of the body must quiet down before sleep can come. (See Chapter 8.)

INSOMNIA

The most common annoyance resulting from excessive tension is insomnia. Inability to sleep is often the first sign of strain and tension. If a person seeks too little sleep, it may be that he is burdened with so many responsibilities or duties he cannot find time to sleep; or he may not value sufficiently the recuperative powers of sleep to make time for it. On the other hand, if an individual cannot sleep when he seeks to do so, it may be because he is too tense and worried.

Although it is difficult to explain physiologically the causes of sleep, it is very simple to explain the cause of insomnia. It depends upon the person's being muscularly and mentally alert. In states of insomnia, the body has to be in some degree of muscular tension. Expecially, when through overwork the muscles have become tense and the brain extremely active, it will take some time before the "wheels will run down." Overactivity during the day, as a result of overaddiction to business, social, or intellectual pursuits, often persists at night in the form of restless and broken sleep. It is a curious fact that the more tense and "worn out" one is physically or mentally the harder it is to get to sleep. Insomnia is not induced by the rhythmic type of exercise, which quickly causes physiologic exhaustion, but by the marked degrees of tonus which accompany mental work and worry—the tonus which goes with attention and held positions. For these reasons, overtense mental workers always complain of insomnia.

It is very difficult to find the proper balance between purposeful work, recreational diversions, and complete cessation of activity.

But such a balance must be maintained if health, vitality, and composure are not to be sacrificed.   Inability to find and maintain this proper proportion between work, diversion, and sleep is the chief cause as well as sign of chronic fatigue and neuromuscular hypertension, with all its accompaniments.   The establishment of a rhythm of living based upon this proportion is essential if one is to have within himself resources for calm disposition, peaceful happiness and health.

3

Physical Factors in Tension and Distress

PHYSICAL AND PSYCHOLOGICAL CAUSES OF FATIGUE AND TENSION

CHRONIC FATIGUE IS DUE to various factors, as many of them physiologic as psychologic. In some cases, it is often difficult to decide which cause is the more fundamental. All of them must be recognized and attacked in order to bring about relief. The only way to treat cases of chronic and excessive tension and stress adequately is to consider physical disturbances and emotional derangements of interrelating importance.

For the past several years, the advice to "consider all factors" has resulted in emphasis upon psychologic and sociologic factors in ill health, probably because these factors were formerly neglected. In considering hypertensive fatigue and resulting discomforts, however, the physiologic factors must still be emphasized because of their important relation to the total problem. It is clearly realized that the individual is a psychophysical organism trying to survive in a hostile social-political-economic environment.

It is tragic how many people suffering from actual excessive tension are called "neurotic" when their difficulties are fundamentally physical. It is also tragic how few people are willing to follow simple techniques for the relief of physical aspects of fatigue. Many laymen who have great respect for organic disease disregard chronic fatigue of the muscular system as a possible cause of serious discomforts.

One must not be too critical of physicians who fall into the easy pattern of dismissing as neurotic cases for which they can find no real pathologic condition, or of giving drugs or recommending hypnosis, when techniques to relax muscles and improved hygiene would be preferable. Their patients often beg them to find organic disease, and insist upon being given drugs instead of following hygienic procedures because they cannot believe that discomforts as great as theirs can be caused by physical indiscretions and unwise living alone. They will take every form of medication on schedule, and yet fail to follow orders for modifications in diet, in exercise, and in daily routine. They cannot believe that their difficulties are due to deficiencies in the muscular tissues or to overuse of those tissues.

One reason why chronic complainers may disregard physical causes of their discomforts or non-medical measures for relief is that they can stimulate themselves with physical aids like coffee or psychological aids like sociability, and cover up symptoms which they would connect with faults in daily hygiene or with "fatigue." Nervous excitability and muscular hypertonus, moreover, they do not associate with overactivity and fatigue. Of course, if they do not connect general unhygienic procedures and hypertensive fatigue with their complaints, they cannot be expected to rely upon improved hygiene and relaxation for relief.

ROLE OF EDUCATION IN RELEASE FROM TENSION

Probably the problem is one for education more than for medicine. Unfortunately, the profession of education has been uncongenial toward those of its members who are interested as much in the body and emotions as in the mind. For many years, classicists in education have excluded from formal education a consideration of the body beautiful or the body in tune with nature, as classicists in medicine have excluded from medical training a strong emphasis upon prophylaxis and prevention of disease. It is often necessary for individuals, on their own initiative, therefore, to plan wisely if their lives are to be directed toward complete psychophysical well-being. Particularly do intellectual workers and those who hold positions of authority need such advice in order to maintain their vitality and to help their bodies release their tensions.

SOURCES OF VITALITY

In order to have life, and to have it abundantly, our resources in vitality and composure must be very high. Our bodies must be elastic, as it were. Our vitality must be rebounding. After a period of exertion we must be able to recuperate quickly and completely, so that we may have energy for the tasks of another day.

No one inherits enough vitality to carry him through his life span. His store of vitality must be replenished each day, through proper nourishment and recuperative rest for the body, and through emotional security and plain common sense for the mind. This is true both of those born with weak constitutions and those born with strong constitutions. Many who are born with weak constitutions impair them further through overwork, worry, dissipation, and illness. However, with proper care, a weak constitution can carry on spectacularly. Without proper care, a magnificent constitution may be wrecked.

INHERENT CONSTITUTION

The matter of inherent constitution, or body type, is very interesting. The anthropologists and students of physique distinguish between two marked types, one called asthenic (weak muscled, and with long spindle-like limbs), and one called hypersthenic (excessively strong, and with chubby, rounded features and limbs). An interpretation of the information accumulated by these scientists, in their study of organic strength and personality through anatomical signs, is that the asthenic type lacks vitality and so becomes easily fatigued and seriously depressed when under strain. It is common knowledge that if a person of this type can get enough rest or gain a little weight, he becomes more contented. The hypersthenic type, on the other hand, has no real lack of vitality, but may burn his candle at both ends "because he likes its lovely light." The candle does burn out, of course, eventually, and he has to give up and rest. Fortunately, the hypersthenic person can recover from overfatigue without too serious consequences, if he rests sufficiently to balance his activity. Even the high blood pressure, from which so many hypersthenic and overactive, sturdy people suffer in later life, may be modified if they can be taught early enough to relax. These individuals must be taught how to balance work with repose and recuperation so that they can continue to have unbounded energy.

It is the asthenic, or very easily fatigued person, however, who interests more the clinician or teacher of health education. He is also very important in our society, because his intelligence is usually high and his nervous drive makes him ingenious, if not stable. This person lives so precariously near the edge of physical incapacity that he is always arousing someone's solicitation. How are we going to recognize this type? The constitutionally asthenic individual, of any age, is to be distinguished by lack of muscular tonus. As indicated above, he tends to be linear in structural dimensions. His chest is long, his waistline small, and his girths around the lower abdomen and upper thighs are greater in proportion than those of the average or sthenic type. He becomes fatigued easily, partly because of his muscular weakness and partly because of his mental alertness or acumen. It is because his mind has to drive such a weak body that he lacks endurance and complains of fatigue.

What causes this asthenic type? One can find very little about constitutional asthenia in medical literature, although transitory forms of asthenia, or "want of vigor" appear in the course of all sorts of systemic diseases, both acute and chronic. Constant forms appear in certain little understood cases of muscular pathology, and in endocrine disturbances. These latter conditions have excited the interest of the medical world, and experiments have been tried with different drugs and with sodium chloride.

As indicated in Chapter 1, the term "neurasthenic" has been bandied about a good deal, but not in a manner to excite the admiration of scientists. A great deal of confusion has arisen because no distinction has been made between true asthenia of the muscular system and weakness of the nervous system, or between "neurasthenias" of biogenic and of psychogenic origins. The type of person whom some physicians have confined to bed and have treated successfully with a combination of rest, isolation, overfeeding, massage, and electrotherapy may not look or act very differently from the person who is psychologically depressed and who will not respond to the same treatment. The latter's initial disturbance is psychological. He may be the returned soldier, who experiences shakiness and exhaustion after emotional upset and intensive exercise, and whose condition is explained by the modern psychotherapist as due to anxiety superimposed on the fear of death or the remembrance of a harrowing experience.

It would be helpful if the average teacher or therapist had a better understanding of these unfortunate individuals who fatigue so easily because of constitutional asthenia, as well as those who have great difficulty in adjusting to their highly stimulating, competitive, and traumatizing environments. There are a great many asthenic as well as neurasthenic workers in the professions, where brains and not brawn are taxed. To say that their many complaints—from cramps in the calves, to gastrointestinal disturbances, to dull pains in the head—are all of psychogenic origin alone is begging the question. Not until we can discover the means of bringing their skeletal musculatures to proper condition can we say that none of the responsibility for their discomforts lies in their neuromuscular systems.

Someday the medical profession may be able to guide asthenic or hypersthenic individuals toward the sthenic or "average" type for body proportions, energy level, and emotional reactions. But no medicine, or surgery, or way of living can make a lean, nervous, high-strung individual permanently over into a stocky, sturdy, easygoing one. Instead of relying upon medicine or surgery or psychiatry to remedy errors which are inherent in our own physiques, we must learn what our constitutions can stand, and we must live within our reserves of energy.

APPRAISING HEALTH ACCOUNTS

Let us think of our constitutions as banks which deal in a medium of exchange more precious than gold or silver. The first deposits to our accounts were made by our forebears. When we get old enough to cash checks we must find out how great is our inheritance. It may be more than we had supposed, or it may be less than we had expected. Great or small, it is all we have to start with. We can cash checks on these banks, but we must make deposits also. As we go through life, we must put back strength into these banks to balance or more than cover what we spend.   Food and rest are our deposits.

It may be necessary in an emergency, or may be fun upon occasion, to spend all we have.   We must know just what our reserves are, however, and be able to replenish the account or it will have to be closed.   None of us need be paupers in energy and few of us can be plutocrats.   But all of us can live within our means and fit our ambitions to our resources or abilities.

Periodically we must appraise our health accounts just as we call for monthly statements at a bank.   When all goes well, the health accounting can be taken care of through routine examinations at a physician's office or at a clinic.   If the examination is thorough, we shall learn whether or not our heart action is normal, whether or not we are anemic, how our kidneys are functioning, what our weight should be, and so on.

If we have an emergency—if we lose too much through gambling away our reserves of strength or through bold enterprise—we may hurry to a specialist who can advise us how to proceed to make up for the losses or expenditures; or we may sit down in privacy and, taking our indiscretions or our responsibilities into account, make a new plan for offsetting the effects of catastrophes.

Every tense individual can find an explanation for his discomforts, if he will honestly appraise his own situation—physically, psychologically, and spiritually, as well as sociologically.   Analysis always necessitates oversimplification by tearing a structure apart and by describing its separate elements.   It is in the scientific spirit of analysis that we now approach this problem of what makes one member of a family less stable than the others, one teacher in a whole school fretful and disliked by the pupils, one lawyer irascible and uncontrolled while his associates remain calm, and one business man in a community suicidal when trade is on the downswing.   Some causes will be physical, some will be psychological.   They will be described, in their more simple aspects, in the following pages.

EXPLANATIONS FROM PHYSIOLOGY AND NEUROLOGY

It is impossible to understand complicated causes of restlessness, of irritability, or of excess tension without understanding the manner

4

in which the body tissues function. The reacting tissues of the body are the glands and the muscles. No matter what influences—external or internal—play upon the body, the glands and muscles are affected. Since it is muscles which become tense, we must have a clear concept of how muscles function normally before we can explain how and why they fail to function properly. When considering structure or anatomy, one may study the various units of the muscular and nervous systems separately; but when considering their functions or physiology, it is impossible to separate muscles from sensory and motor nerves, spinal cord and brain, and to assign to each a separate role. Functionally the nervous and muscular systems are one.

RESPONSE TO STIMULATION

Nerves and muscles must respond when they are stimulated. The sensory field from which impulses come is very wide. Some nerve cells bring messages from the outside of the body, through the senses of touch, sight, hearing, taste, and smell. These are called exteroceptive. Others bring messages from the internal organs of the abdominal and pelvic cavities, and are called interoceptive. Still others bring messages from the muscles, tendons, and joints. They are called proprioceptive, meaning activated by, pertaining to or designating stimuli produced within the self. In the spinal cord and brain, all these messages from the sensorium are coordinated and are sent out over another set of nerve cells to the glands and muscles to make them function. Furthermore, every nerve cell carrying impulses to the spinal cord and brain has potential connections with every nerve cell carrying impulses away. A stimulus received anywhere in the sensorium, therefore, may excite gland or muscle cells to activity.

An example of response of a muscular organ within the body to an external stimulus is the increase in the rate of the heart beat when one hears a shriek. An example of response in the muscles which move the body to an internal stimulus is the stiffening of the whole body in a bent position on experiencing a sharp pain in the stomach.

We are to understand that, when any part of the sensory nervous system is stimulated, a muscular contraction or a glandular reaction

will take place. We become fatigued because glands go on functioning and muscles go on contracting just because the sensorium is being
stimulated. The active glandular response is secretion. The active
muscular response is always contraction. It is when no impulse car-
ries over from the nerve to the muscle that there is a negative or
passive response—relaxation. So long as we are awake, and seeing
and hearing, nerve messages are passing to our muscles and glands.
Whenever our digestive organs are taking care of food or, particularly, when any internal organ is functioning improperly so that
there is pressure on interoceptive nerve endings, excitations must
pass to reacting tissues. Whenever there is pressure or pain in a
contracting muscle or in a joint, messages must go to glands and
other muscles, smooth, cardiac and striated.

The more exciting or exacting the external environmental conditions, the more fatiguing they are to the muscular system. The more
disturbed the internal enviroment becomes, the more unfavorably it
reacts on the organism. This explanation is one to justify periodic
sleep or repose, when stimuli can be cut down and the body can
become rested.

Most activity of the human body is not conscious, but reflexive.
Of interest, in connection with a study of cumulative fatigue, are
certain reflexes—automatic responses in the muscles to stimuli of the
sensorium—operating during most of our waking hours. For example, experiments have shown that the physical fact which causes
contraction of muscle is the "stretch reflex." Whenever a muscle is
slightly stretched, the sensory nerve endings in its sheath are stimulated, and send impulses to the central nervous system, which in
turn relays them to the muscles concerned, causing contraction
against the load which was responsible for the stretching. The weight
of individual parts of the body, succumbing to the force of gravity,
is enough to cause contraction in individual muscles in response to
their stretch. Just sitting or standing against the pull of gravity, for
example, causes muscular contraction or tension, as everyone has
experienced. Such simple physical acts as reading and writing,
when the head and trunk are inclined forward, will make one
fatigued if they are persisted in too long at one period. Organized
thinking is a cumulative trauma that must be interrupted by rest.

Many other simple reflex contractions follow stimuli to the sense organs on the outside of the body, in the internal organs, and in the muscle sheaths and joint spaces. It has been discovered experimentally that these stimuli augment one another, a fact which explains physiologically why a person becomes excited and hypertense if he is stimulated too much by sights, noises, cramping positions, and pain particularly. It is this augmentation, or piling up of muscular contractions when the body is acted upon by too many external or internal stimuli, that is one of the causes of overuse of the muscles and glands, and of consequent fatigue. If a person lets himself be played upon by too many stimuli, he must expect to become tense and fatigued.

BREAKDOWN IN MUSCLE TISSUE

Substances within the muscle tissue are broken down during contraction. The wear and tear of a machine are entirely due to the frictional forces between materials which have no relation to the fuel of such a machine. In the living cell, however, structure and fuel are essentially similar materials, and no wear and tear can take place without changes in the structure of the machine. In living tissues the changes are chemical.

The changes in muscle tissues may be explained somewhat as follows. Upon stimulation, an unstable compound, named "phosphagen," breaks down into creatine and phosphoric acid. During contraction and relaxation in the next few minutes, lactic acid is set free by the breakdown of glycogen or animal starch, with a liberation of heat. The conversion of glycogen into lactic acid during muscular work is a non-oxidative reaction and occurs irrespective of the presence or absence of oxygen. In fact, a muscle will continue to contract for an appreciable time in the complete absence of oxygen, because of the fact that lactic acid is quickly neutralized by certain alkaline bicarbonates, phosphates, and alkaline salts of the muscle proteins, known collectively as the muscle buffers. Apparently, oxygen is used after the exertion is over, in effecting a restoration of the system to its previous condition. There has to be a relaxation phase in every muscle twitch or contraction, as well as a period of rest after every bout of effort to bring about recovery.

RECOVERY FROM OXYGEN DEBT

Any circulatory or respiratory deficiency which restricts the availability of oxygen delays recuperation from exertion, since oxygen is the essential need during the recovery phase. In listing the limiting factors in fatigue of an organic nature, investigators place oxygen supply and the rate at which oxygen may be supplied to local areas before supply of glycogen or poor neuromuscular coordination necessitating excess expenditure of energy.

An increase in oxygen intake is essential during all forms of muscular activity and in the periods necessary for recuperation. During brief rest pauses or during longer periods of cessation from action, the body has an opportunity to cancel its oxygen debt, as it were. The demand for oxygen in the muscular tissues is met both by an increase in the rate and strength of the heart beat, and by a relaxation in the tissues themselves and an expanding of the capillaries to permit the oxygen to get to the cells which need it, as well as by an increase in the rate and depth of respiration. In the later discussion of forms of treatment for excess muscular tension and fatigue, a great deal of emphasis will be placed upon techniques for improving the circulation and for increasing chest action.

We are to understand, then, that the neuromuscular system becomes fatigued because food materials in the muscles are used up or changed chemically and because toxins accumulate in the muscles. Physiologically speaking, fatigue results when muscles do not contain the proper energy-giving materials and do not get enough oxygen to take care of the end-products of muscular work. Physiologically, then, all that is needed to prevent fatigue is to supply proper nutrients to the muscles and to provide for the removal of products of muscular contraction. Proper food, proper exercise, and proper rest are our physical bulwarks against fatigue.

NUTRIMENT

Food, its type and quantity, has a great influence on vitality. Until recently, nutrition was only an art, but now it is gradually becoming a science. Among some peoples, like the Italians and the Chinese, the artist cooks have always provided very substantial as well as attractive menus for their wealthy patrons. But the diets of most nationalities have not been adequate in kind and the food intake has been deficient either in quantity or in quality for the common man. As the science of nutrition becomes better formulated and more conscientiously adhered to in practice, the vigor of all races will be greatly increased.

At the present stage of experimentation in nutrition, most of the advice that can be given comes under the heading of "common sense." There are three general rules to be followed: First, eat the quantity and kind of foods which maintain your weight uniformly close to a level which you can honestly acknowledge as associated with your feeling most fit. Second, eat as great a variety of foods as possible. Third, select foods in their natural or unrefined states.

Do not be influenced by diet fads for reducing. Extreme dieting should be supervised by a physician or a technically trained specialist. Pills or concentrates recommended to augment the diet and purported to give pep or to control weight should be taken only under the strict supervision of a physician. Substances to assist in reducing or in gaining are really medications, and should never be taken except under a doctor's prescription. And that prescription should be given for the very person taking the "cure," not for his uncle, or his mother's friend, or his next-door neighbor, Do not fall into the habit of so many nervous and uncomfortable people—self-medication. Try instead, to eat sanely.

To lose weight may mean to lose strength. Do not fail to get sufficient carbohydrates and calcium. In investigations under everyday working conditions, tests of capacity, speed, endurance, and muscular coordination seem to bring out the fact that low sugar content in a diet impairs efficiency. One should be warned against the current fad of reducing by eliminating sugars and starches (from which sugars are manufactured in the body itself). It is to be understood that this suggestion does not justify an abnormal increase in sugar intake. Too much is as bad as too little.

Of all food items, the one which has received the approval of all time and of all people is milk. The calcium in milk helps to maintain proper conditions in nervous and muscular tissue, as well as to assist in the growth of skeleton and teeth. Many individuals revealing marked hypertonus have not been accustomed to a generous amount of milk each day.   In at least all cases of localized muscle soreness of long duration, calcium therapy should be instituted. (Sun therapy as a means of assisting calcium metabolism has its place in the treatment of all cases of faulty responsiveness of the nervous and muscular tissues.   Is it possible that one reason why many individuals become irritable and restless in the late winter is because the ultraviolet rays of the sun have been reduced for many months, and because the calcium metabolism of the body has been reduced accordingly?)

When it is possible to get nature's products in nature's form, it is only sensible to take them without refinement or modification.   Only in emergencies—during illness or during social crises, when proper foodstuffs are not available   is it wise or economical to eat artificially.

If one believes that nature is serving the body and soul, one will be more inclined to select foods as they come from nature.   Unfortunately, as civilization has tended in the direction of nonessentials and artificiality, there has been a tendency toward "refining" and "clarifying" foods.   The essentials have been taken out of grains and cereals, for example; and the appearance of many foods has been enhanced by ornamentation and fancy coloring.

All over the world people of "refinement" prefer white flour or polished rice, thus depriving themselves of the essential vitamins and minerals which are to be found only in the casings.   To be sure, recently, there has been a crusade for returning some minerals and the vitamins, in concentrated form, to the flour after it has been "refined" for fastidious tastes.   This procedure of removing essentials and then returning them in magnified quantity seems fantastic. There can be no wisdom in removing the essentials, in the beginning, and of educating the palates of so-called healthy people to prefer denuded food materials.

Eating enough different things will provide a balanced diet.   This advice comes directly from Prof. Elmer V. McCollum, one of the investigators who contributed most to the modern science of nutrition.   As his associates discovered or isolated a new vitamin or basic mineral in some food, McCollum did not urge everyone to start consuming quantities of that food.   His advice, from the beginning of his investigations, was to sample anything that is to be found in the best local market or first-rate restaurant. If you eat everything nature has to give, you will be getting the most balanced diet she has to offer.

No sympathy should be wasted on the fussy eater. It may be the initial fault of his parents that he does not like certain things, but it is his responsibility to put away childish characteristics when he becomes a man. If one wishes to have a life of thrills and temptations, why exclude stimulations to taste? If one wishes to have a life of balance and variation, why neglect the culinary arts? Think what is missed in the way of excitement to the palate in refusing to sample new dishes and concoctions that may seem strange! To be a glutton may be a vice, but to be a connoisseur of good food is never so. It may not be deleterious to health to miss ripe olives and cardamon seeds and anchovy paste; but it is really unfortunate not to get yellow squash and cheese and soy beans. It is foods like the latter that fussy eaters refuse to sample. Some of these foods, like the squash, are rich in an essential vitamin; and the cheese and soy beans, for example, are rich in calcium.

Every food has something to offer to the one who must make of it his body and his energy. There is much to be said in favor of the simple concept of the Eastern philospoher who argues in this way: "Yesterday, my food was under the ground, in the water, or free in the sunshine, rain or wind. Today, it enters my body and becomes my flesh. Tomorrow, all but the residue comes forth in the form of actions and ideas. Eventually this body of mine returns to the soil, to the water, and to the air."

FLUID INTAKE

Many chronically tense people do not drink much water. They would feel better if they did. A practical hint for well-being has always been to drink water after work or physical exertion in order to feel refreshed. This simple procedure serves a real body need. The function of the water is both to assist in physiochemical processes and to keep the by-products of muscular work in sufficient solution. As is well known, deprivation of liquid intake as well as loss of blood, resulting in an inadequate volume in the circulatory vessels, rapidly causes exhaustion. Forms of effort demanding tonic contraction of muscles over a long period of time actually increase the need for water. Observedly, tensions accompanying accentuated emotional states do so also. We are all accustomed to the dryness of the lips and tongue and the distressing thirst which accompany fear and anxiety.

During accentuated emotional states, as well as during strenuous physical exertion, perspiration is increased sufficiently to effect a lowering of fluid in the body. There are probably other physiologic causes as well for loss of fluid during mental or emotional exertion. It is known that, in human subjects, mental or emotional stimuli which bring about reflex postural patterning of the skeletal muscles may cause, also, reflex tonic contraction of the "smooth" sphincter muscle of the bladder, thus necessitating frequent urinating.

It has been suggested that taking mildly saline solutions will markedly increase the retention of water in the body, and will offset the development of fatigue. As a case to demonstrate the desirability of maintaining the fluid content of the body by this expedient there is the experience of a man on a salt-free diet. His sweating became more pronounced, he easily lost appetite, on the fifth day he experienced extreme lassitude, on the eighth and ninth days he suffered from muscular soreness and stiffness, and then from muscular twitchings.

This does not mean that everyone should immediately drink a glassful of strong salt solution, but it is advised that no one refrain from salting his food, a little, unless a physician has advised otherwise. When about to take part in a strenuous activity one might take a drink of mild salty water, as many athletes and manual workers do. It is known definitely that the intake of the salts of sodium, calcium, and potassium—the fixed bases—assist the buffer action of the body fluids to offset an increase in lactic acid during muscular activity.

Any discussion concerning the lack of wisdom on the part of so-called educated people is always entertaining to the one initiating it. Why not take up the argument where it now lies, and carry it into your own home or office? Why not decide that you, at least, are going to eat according to a few sound principles, and not according to the dictates of your jaded or unintelligent palate? You will drink a great deal of milk. You will start to use brown bread and brown sugar. You will get a great variety of vegetables, and eat them raw or with the very water in which they were cooked. You will eat every kind of meat. You will not have to follow any special diet or to take extra capsules or tablets in order to reinforce your meals. You will not have to select bulky foods or take roughage, because none of your foods will be concentrated. Yet none of them will be indigestible. You will not refuse to season your food. In fact, you may add a variety of spices in order to increase the mineral content of your food and encourage yourself to drink a lot of water. Of course you will not eliminate salt for the same reasons. If you take wine or beer, it will be as part of your meals. If you take anything hot to drink, it will be when you frankly want a stimulant. In other words, you will eat and drink to give yourself strength and vigor, beauty, and virility. If you are well, you will not be eating to "get fat" or to "get thin." If you should be fatter or if you should be thinner, you are not well, and should be under the care of a physician.

Fatness and thinness are complicated and quite individual matters, decided by family type and by personal rate of metabolism. They depend only partly upon the intake of food. We know that they are not absolutely associated with excitability nor with relaxability. Of course some people lose appetite when they are under strain; others overindulge in food when they are unhappy. It is not appropriate, however, to discuss diets for gaining or for reducing in a book on neuromuscular fatigue and its relief. All that can be said is that if either gaining or losing makes one feel better, it should be encouraged; whereas when weight is a burden, it should be discarded and when thinness means lack of vigor, it should be modified. Dieting according to the simple rule of selecting a variety of products directly from nature will not encourage undesirable gaining or losing.

EXERCISE

Exercise must share the responsibility, with eating, for personal physical fitness. Exercise, as well as diet, must be taken into consideration in any scheme for individual, national or racial fitness.

Everyone needs to find some vigorous occupation, preferably out-doors. Lucky is the farmer, mason, or woodcutter whose employ-ment takes him into many kinds of weather. Fortunate is the woman who has a garden. Fortunate is the man who has a boat. Fortunate, also, are the people who have a chance to walk b ack and forth to work every day. Sensible are the others who find a way, through outdoor sports or through camping and hiking, to get their share of physical activity in various kinds of weather.

Those who are determined to preserve the robust, virile side of their beings must not be dissuaded by so-called philosophers, who preach that man is now a more intellectual being than he was when he had to run and climb and dig for his living, and that it is puerile, if not imbecile, to try to revive the out-of-date body of primitive man. One can answer from medical and psychiatric case studies of highly intellectual beings who have broken down and been unable to live out their chosen life roles because of neglect of the body. This is no place to make a plea for strenuous gymnastics or athletics, out of all proportion to the other phases of living; it is a place to make a plea for a reasonable amount of wholesome activity, to be continued throughout life, to offset the tensions and frustrations of a mechan-ized, economically competitive, and socially unsatisfying existence.

There is no lack of specialists in physical education to help earnest seekers after a balanced way of life. Muscle strength, however, is not a consideration in ability to relax. Therefore, powerful weight-lifting tricks are of no account. Gymnasiums filled with gadgets for developing and testing muscle power are as useless for developing ability to relax as they are for developing social traits.

To be sure, men who are proud of their muscles will say that they can relax best after they have had a "workout" with the bar bells or medicine ball, and they place the credit for the relief from strain upon the strength-giving exercises. They forget that they have taken time away from work, have undressed, have chatted with gym-nasium attendants and rubbers, have had a good massage and a long shower, and have been forced to forget their worries. Had they left on their clothes, had they worked on the biceps of the arm and quadriceps of the leg at their own offices near the telephones, had they hurried back to their desks without a shower or a drink, they would not have been refreshed. No, it is not strengthening exercises which relax a body.

Ability to beat another at a given task is not of the essence of relaxation, so competitive activities have no particular share in a program to counteract tension and encourage composure. In fact, there is considerable evidence to support the contention that the tremendous urge toward competition is one of the reasons why excitability and irritability are so ingrained in modern society. An exercise regime to encourage ability to relax, in an individual or in a people, would never be built on the principle of competition. No, exercise for relaxation is not competitive and it is not for the purpose of building strength. As far as physical exercise goes, it must smooth out the tight places in the body, not make more of them. It must upset held positions, not add poses of attention. It must counteract alertness, not keep a person keyed up.

However, there are psychological advantages to competition and strenuous exercise, when they are of a recreational nature. Recreation can be envisioned as a state of mind attained through all-absorbing activity in which one can lose onself. The activity does not have to be strictly physical, but it may be.

In fact, physical activity in the form of athletics and team games has been associated, in all ages, with the release of pent up emotions— religious, sexual and patriotic. Although this release may take the form of unseemly conduct at times, and may bring social opposition to sports and sportsmen, upon occasion, it must be credited with affording the participants some degree of mental and emotional relaxation. One does not even have to be a participant in the contest or on the team to get some benefit; one may be having a vicarious experience as a spectator. It is generally recognized that in modern times the wide interest of Anglo-Saxon masses in horse racing, football, baseball and similar sports tends to allay social unrest and lessens the possibility of political uprisings. Visions of Rome in the days of Nero!

In colleges and universities in the United States, athletics have been promoted as much to offer recreation or relaxation from mental strain and to prepare the students with a means of relieving the deleterious effects of the machine age, as to encourage them to strive for and to value physical fitness. Would that they were generally required now, as they used to be; and that more young people threw their energies into them! The ideals of physical training in the United States embrace keeping the physical activities in schools and colleges on a fun or amateur, and therefore on a relaxing level, in contrast to a professional or highly competitive plane.

The principles governing exercises for relaxing can be clearly defined. Some movements should be rhythmic but not too strenuous. Others may afford a more deliberate alternation between complete stretch of a muscle and complete release of the tautness. Still others must distort the body so that the joints are moved through their full ranges of motion. In Chapter 5 will be found specific suggestions for mild rhythmic motions, for stretches to be followed by release of tautness, and for distorted positions to increase mobility in joints. In that chapter emphasis will also be placed on techniques for relaxation in the muscle tissues themselves, by reducing spasm in the fibers and by improving the circulation in the affected areas.

PAIN IN RELATION TO TENSION

In the previous chapter, pain was considered a sign of muscular tension. It may be a cause, also. When muscles are tense and circulation is impeded, discomfort is always an accompaniment. Apparently, muscular spasm and oxygen want in localized areas are important contributory causes of the pain and the inflammatory conditions of joints and nerves as well as muscles. The muscular tension must be released before the circulation can pass unrestricted, and the pain can abate. Any improvement in circulation, therefore, brought about by heat, massage, mild rhythmic exercise, or conscious relaxation will release the pain and the tension at the same time.

In discussing pain, it will be necessary to distinguish between different possible sources. When a physician has diagnosed arthritis, neuritis, or myositis—imflammation of joints, nerves, and muscles, respectively—it will be necessary to acknowledge this explanation for the pain. When the individual has had acute or chronic injury, the specific consequences of the violence or static strain must be recognized and relieved. Apparently, whenever any part of the body is wrenched, the muscles in that region contract tonically to prevent more pain. The reaction is purely reflexive. The spasmodic contractions of muscles following an acute injury may be localized or widespread in the body and are likely to persist longer than necessary to save the injured part from jarring.

Arthritis, neuritis, and myositis are not subjects to be discussed in detail in a non-medical book. They are conditions of great interest to physiotherapists and teachers of corrective exercise, however, because so many physicians are turning to these technicians to help them in relieving the symptoms of their patients, while they are trying to discover the causes of the pathology.

While discussing arthritis, in fairness to the most recent work on that subject, it must be recalled that scientific investigators and physicians have recognized a relationship between the symptoms of chronic arthritis and "nervousness." Anyone who has been troubled with joint pain of indefinite origin should take very seriously suggestions for the counteracting of psychological as well as physical causes of "nervousness," tension, and fatigue.

When other causes of pain have been eliminated, it will be necessary to consider the possibilities of increased sensitivity as the result of increased muscular tension alone. Finally, it will become important to decide whether or not there may be a series of factors associated with pain in a vicious circle. For may not such conditions as arthritis and trauma increase residual tension sufficiently to cause more pain than the original lesion warrants? Will the tensions developed with the bearing of any pain increase the pain? Or may muscular tension by itself, from any other cause, bring about symptoms like those usually ascribed to inflammation and injury?

Whereas arthritis, neuritis, and myositis which are the results of pathological conditions in the body as a whole are very hard to counteract and to cure, joint, nerve, and muscle involvements from specific injuries are easier to explain and treat.

When one considers chronic, static strain, in contrast to acute injury, he is impressed even more with the close relationship between residual muscular tension and pain. The usual acute injury has as its most serious consequences actual bone fractures, joint dislocations and ligamentous tears. The muscular spasms come as a consequence of a reflex reaction which represents mechanisms to keep the segments immobile in order to prevent joint irritation. Most chronic or static strain, on the other hand, involves the muscles primarily. For example, when feet or back are subjected to static strain, because of habitual poor posture or superimposed weight, the strain is usually felt first in the muscles. Only when the muscles give up their burden does the pain become localized in specific joints.

Regions of the body which exhibit most static strain, in business and professional people, in society matrons and housewives, and in students, are the neck and lower back. These "workers" all try to keep their heads and trunks erect or in set poses for too many hours every day. Whenever an individual asks what may be done to relieve pain at the nape of the neck or in the lower back, the answer should be, "Spend more time in bed at night, and lie down occasionally during the day, so that the muscles may be relieved of effort and the neck and back may become rested."

A circumstance which aggravates the muscular condition following all acute injuries seems to be fear of being hurt again. Even when an injury is given the best possible orthopedic care, there is some pain. Naturally, the victim does not wish to experience that sensation again.

It is easy to understand the manner in which fear of recurring pain can cause tonic muscular contraction. It is less easy to understand how other fear states may have the same consequences, although observation supports the contention that they do. All fears arrest movement and cause residual muscular hypertonus. Fears set the individual against his environment physically as well as psychologically. (See Chapter 4.)

In summarizing the interrelationships between pain and residual tension, certain definite principles should be stated. Although pain is perceived by the brain—the highest part of the nervous system, it is received by the sensory nerve endings—the lowest part of that same system. Although it may appear to the unsympathetic observer that the pain is highly exaggerated, it must still be accepted as having a physical basis. Furthermore, tonic contraction of muscles, made in an effort to prevent movement following acute trauma or to prevent recurrence of chronic pain, will cause enough increased irritability to contribute more pain. It is desirable, therefore, to relieve initial pain whenever it occurs, and to keep strained muscles relaxed. An efficient method for getting rid of much pain appears to be to relax it away.

In Chapter 5 on the Physical Methods of Relaxing, mention will be made of drugs and other medical devices to bring about blessed unconsciousness when suffering is unbearable.

POSTURES AS CAUSES OF TENSENESS

In Chapter 2 on signs of excess muscular tension mention was made of rigid postures, with their accompanying discomforts, and awkward movements marking the tense man. There was an implication that these restrictions in movement are causes of further tension and discomfort. Why? Because they demand excess muscular work.

In order to bring about coordinated movements and held attitudes, it is necessary for muscles not only to move segments of the skeleton, but to hold segments stationary. In other words, muscles may contract in response to stimulation, or they may maintain a contraction in response to stimulation. The first form of action is called "phasic" or "kinetic" contraction; the second is called "tonic," "static," or "postural" contraction. Both forms are seen more and more clearly to rest upon the same essential integrated activity of muscle and nerve.

As to the physical changes occurring in tonically and phasically contracting muscles, there seem to be no differences except in the degree of shortening of the fibers. As to the chemical changes, tonic contraction as well as phasic produces the same metabolites. When tonic contraction is done powerfully, as in such an activity as heavy weight lifting, it is very demanding, causes changes in the breathing and necessitates long rest pauses between bouts of effort. In fact, this type of exercise is the most effective for getting the greatest physiologic "workout" in the shortest time. Athletic sports which have in them held positions and sustained effort against external force—like rowing—are also very strenuous.

The amount of tonic contraction which is incorporated into the average activities of each day may not cause discomfort. But if we are asked to hold a specific position until we are "tired," we become conscious of doing "work." It is this type of muscular contraction, too long sustained, from which we may have to learn to relax. For example, if we sit at our desks for short periods of time separated by periods of moving about, we do not get tired; but, if we sit in one posture for hours at a time without any interruptions, the muscles of our back and neck get very tense and sore. It is this static type of muscular effort of which many of the people who are reading this book have cause to complain. They may never have thought of their lives as being muscularly strenuous, but the held positions which they have maintained during periods of diversion as well as during hours of work have been tensing to the muscular system.

MENTAL WORK AND MUSCULAR TENSENESS

Mental work is particularly tensing. What is pure mental work? According to the James-Lange theory, thought and emotions are always reflected upon the muscles, which in turn react and return impulses to the brain. It has been said that we "think" with the muscles, because every thought is accompanied by muscular contraction and every muscular contraction arouses some feeling.

Most of the muscular activity associated with mental work is of the tonic type and is exhibited in arrested movement and increased attention. Attention is definitely a muscular phenomenon. The very attitude of anyone who expectantly awaits a sound or a signal— the movements of his head and the expression of his face—shows that attention is closely connected with motor phenomena. Usually, when an intellectual effort is made, there is a slight but definite forward posturing of the head which lasts for the duration of the effort. The bowed head observable in certain people when thinking deeply is obviously an exaggeration of this reflex.

Increases in tonus which states of attention affect are not localized in the neck, but are widespread in the body. Besides the head and trunk being held statically during attention, respiratory movements are definitely impeded because of increased tonus of the diaphragm and other muscles of respiration. It is interesting that every individual seems to develop with all his efforts definite patterns of tonic contraction in other parts of the body.

Since mental effort makes slight demands upon the physiologic stores in the muscles and develops few toxic end-products, it can be carried on for long stretches of time without much rest. It is the simple fact that mental fatigue never leaves the stage of neuromuscular hypertension for the stage of exhaustion that makes it so annoying and disastrous. Furthermore, mental processes seem always to be associated with emotional striving. Therefore, they goad the body on to endeavor far beyond its strength.

The most productive minds have been subject to fatigue quite readily. We are told that to Darwin and to Zola work for more than three hours daily was an impossibility, and yet their work done under these restrictions excites all men's admiration. These men knew that their mental powers would serve them adequately if only they heeded the warnings of fatigue, and gave themselves diversion and sufficient rest. Slight mental fatigue, on the other hand, should not cause anyone too much concern if he knows how to offset it sufficiently to get periodic recuperation. It is a matter of planning wisely.

INSOMNIA IN ITS RELATION TO HYPERACTIVITY

One of the worst features of mental work is that it may keep an individual in a state of neuromuscular hypertension late in the evening, thus preventing sleep. Just as insomnia could be described in the previous chapter as one of the most common signs of overfatigue and excessive tension, it can be described, also, as a cause of more activity with resulting fatigue. Insomnia invariably increases mental as well as muscular tension to a high level. The first effects of fatigue through loss of sleep are further stimulation of the mental powers and emotional instability, as well as muscular hypertension. It has been demonstrated repeatedly that actual mental efficiency is not reduced after many hours of going without sleep, possibly as a result of interest in what the mind is grappling with or of increased effort, or of the normal phase of hyperexcitability in the fatigue syndrome. Instead, it usually is increased until an inability to fix the attention develops, and the individual becomes peevish and irritable.

PHYSICAL CAUSES OF PSYCHOLOGICAL DISTRESS

Too much emphasis cannot be placed upon the fact that many mental workers try to exist on rations of sleep which are far below the necessary minimum. Because mental work tends to drive one to a stage of hyperexcitability, the mental worker feels alert and is inclined to scrimp on sleep. When he lives on a minimum of sleep, he is constantly in a stage of physiologic as well as psychologic hypertension, which in turn will carry the body toward eventual breakdown. A vicious circle is easily set up through which the sleeplessness caused by hyperactivity and refusal to go to sleep can intensify the hyperexcitability and lead to more insomnia.

4

Psychological Factors Causing Neuromuscular Hypertension

RELATION OF PHYSICAL AND PSYCHOLOGICAL CONDITIONS

WHEN ONE IS PHYSICALLY RELAXED one is less irritable emotionally; when one is psychologically calm one is not tense physically. No topic is more helpful in explaining psychosomatic relationships than relaxation—its causes, consequences and methods of achievement. The previous chapter emphasized the relationship of physical indiscretions to tension and stress.

Physicians recognize emotional disturbances and intellectual strivings, as well as neuromuscular behavior, in the causation of stress. Sometimes they emphasize one and sometimes another if they have a difficult patient. But if the tension is not too extreme, they often recommend mild physical activity. Psychologists and psychiatrists also often advocate physical activity for the anxieties which are the psychological antithesis of relaxation. However, their more direct methods of counselling and insight therapy have to be used also for deeply disturbed persons.

It may be possible to divert one's mind by physical activity, but one cannot expect to modify the aberrant behavior which accompanies severe stress and to offset the lowering of intellectual control, attention and concentration which accompany anxiety, by physical activity alone. It has to be accompanied by understanding and will to change. However, no psychiatric therapy could work today without physical activities to occupy part of the patient's time while he is being helped to give up his strivings and to achieve self-discipline. For the degree of tension which every one of us experiences, this device of physical activity is worth enjoying.

In studying the previous chapter, the student probably realized that games and sports have frequently been used to help a person relax, mainly because of the common observation that an athlete looks relaxed during performance and in his free time. But an athlete appears relaxed because his movements are efficient. He makes no extraneous motions. On the other hand, because of his skills, the athlete feels sure of himself, and therefore is calm. As was said of Joe Louis, who had an enviable reputation for being relaxed, "he knew that if he was better than the other fighter, and didn't make too many mistakes, he would win."* But remember that after his performances, as for any athlete, there was always stock taking and planning for a subsequent contest.

The individual who has participated with enjoyment in the type of physical activity which induces relaxation, just for fun, is refreshed intellectually and calmed down emotionally. He may not be able to concentrate immediately afterwards on the problem which he was attacking before his diversion, but after a brief time he will find that the fun-filled physical diversion served as a rest pause to increase his efficiency. We have all had the experience of having an idea flash into mind when we have stopped struggling to recall it, or after a period of repose.

There have been many reports of personal regimens which support these general observations regarding the effects of physical diversion as well as more direct techniques in relaxation upon emotional and intellectual behavior. It is known that, in order to be relaxed during a period of stress, Theodore Roosevelt and Thomas Edison, both men of action, took catnaps. Eleanor Roosevelt was reported as taking short rests before she got tired. To keep relaxed during a race, Paava Nurmi carried a watch, for he insisted on running his own race, keeping his own tempo, and never hurrying.

* Kennedy, Joseph A. *Relax and Live.* New York: Prentice-Hall, 1953, p. 112.

And isn't it true that, throughout the world, men in the armed forces and manual laborers have always performed to music in order that their fatigue might be less?

When one is physically relaxed, to be sure, one is also relaxed emotionally and intellectually. And if one performs any task without worry or overeffort, in a relaxed manner, one does not work "into a stew" that keeps one keyed up after the event.

PSYCHIC CAUSES OF GENERALIZED TENSIONS

Generalized tensions in the body are as likely to be psychological as physical in origin; and emotional problems must take their share of responsibility for increased neuromuscular reactions. Just as fatigue from physical causes makes one more irritable and "nervous," mental states associated with anxiety, fear, depression, despair, and prolonged conflict cause physical disorders revealing tenseness.

It is to be observed that motility, sensitivity, and secretion, as well as emotion, perception, memory, and thought, are all manifestations of activity of the various psychologic as well as physiologic levels of the nervous system. Since the psychologic level is the highest in functional importance, it is not difficult to understand how disturbances on that level can upset all other levels of the nervous system.

INSECURITY AND COMPULSION

The psychologic factors which seem to make adults more tense may be grouped under two major headings: insecurity leading to fears and worries, and compulsion leading to over-effort and hurry. They show in everything the tense individual does.

One of the fundamental causes of both insecurity and compulsion is self-centeredness. Hypertense individuals, almost without exception, are "hyperselfly" individuals. In some instances they give the appearance of being self-sufficient: in others they show every sign of conscious or unconscious inferiority. Their self-interest exhibits itself in their relation with other individuals. In fact, the conflict of the "self" with social forces reacting upon it or the competition of the "self" with other "selves" causes the insecurity which compels individuals to over-effort and sustained tension.

THWARTING OF LIFE'S PURPOSES

When we approach the problems of why and how the self may be propelled toward over-effort and disturbance, we acknowledge that there are four great drives which motivate and sustain an individual person as well as a social group—work, play, love, and worship. If there is no conflict between desire and achievement in these realms, the individual or the society is untroubled and "healthy." If the individual or his society fails to acknowledge any one of these drives, or places undue stress on one to the sacrifice of the others, that individual or that society becomes distorted and finally ineffectual. Life must be balanced between work, play, love, and worship. While each must be pursued for its inherent satisfactions, all must have a chance to react upon each other. To maintain maximum output in work, one must spend some time in play, must attain satisfaction in love, and at the same time grow in spiritual power. Work, play, love, and worship contribute to a balanced way of living and to a framework for personality which keeps the individual calm and poised as well as dynamic. It is just as important to balance these drives in times of stress as in periods of quiet.

ADJUSTMENT TO WORK

No life is complete and satisfying without work. Webster's dictionary begins its definition of "work" with these words, "Exertion of strength or faculties to accomplish something," and continues with an amazing list of projects including a book or poem, embroidery or needlework, docks and bridges, moral duties and ceremonial acts. "Work," then, is the general term for purposive effort. Labor, toil, and drudgery—words often considered synonyms of work—imply strenuous, fatiguing or distasteful effort. Work, however, need not be unpleasant. Work is just what has to be done. If the task at hand is one for which the worker is adequately prepared, and one from which he knows he will gain rewards commensurate with his effort, he will expend his energies willingly and to the limit, with the minimum of strain. This fact accounts for the magnificent output of people during an emergency.

Everyone knows physicians who have gone without adequate sleep for days during a catastrophe or serious epidemic, lawyers who have worked continuously through the night getting briefs ready, authors and editors who have had to push themselves to shape up manuscripts by publication date, parents who have gone without rest or sustenance at the bed-side of a sick child, etc., etc. Not all these efforts take on an aspect of heroism, but many such are essential to the orderly running of corporate life. Yet, work of this quality or work of less social significance cannot be maintained at excessive intensity or tempo except under the goad of tremendous emotion.

The emotional goad for much over-effort in work is not altruism, but the same self-centeredness which has been stressed as the fundamental cause of both insecurity and compulsion. Throughout this discussion of the psychological factors in fatigue and excess tension, self-centeredness will repeatedly rear its ugly head. Self-centeredness is revealed by many forms of behavior.

A few years ago, a cultured young Belgian doctor, resident for a year in the United States, was asked how he would characterize an American. His answer was, "An American woman wants to be married to the leading citizen of her town or to be acknowledged as its best informed and most philanthropically minded citizen. Her man wants to make more money than anyone else in the town. Their child is their master."

FINANCIAL GOALS

The man wants to make money. With rare exceptions, the financial goal has seemed more important than any other. It is this goal which leads to material progress, so-called; but it can also lead to heartbreaks and to hypertensive psychophysical disorders. Although ambition leads to enterprise, it rarely leads to composure. The person who desires, above all things, to make money must do so at the sacrifice of many other life values and life rewards. He must believe that he cannot take time for diversion and periodic relaxation. He must participate in cutthroat competition. Even with the amount of money that brings security come unlimited responsibilities which, in many instances, bring further worries.

PROFESSIONAL ADVANCEMENT

Everyone knows individuals who drive themselves for prestige or preferment, without financial considerations. These drives are neither more nor less acceptable than financial ones. The implication is not that these goads to overwork are unworthy. They are just demanding. Examples of non-financial drives are not hard to find in science, where technicians labor unstintingly on their experiments; or in education, where the pressure to become acknowledged as an authority is particularly impelling. They are not hard to find in other professions, in politics, in business.

Wherever people are desperately seeking economic, educational, professional, or social advancement, there will be found dissatisfied individuals who are constantly in a state of hyperactivity and hypertension. No situation is more pregnant with possibilities for psychophysical breakdown than one where many individuals are struggling for self-advancement and recognition, sometimes beyond their abilities, in the highly competitive environment which we call progressive modern society. Self-advanceemnt is a cruel master and many of its slaves suffer more acutely from its lashings than the human slaves of earlier cultures. The fallacy is that we think we each can be masters of ourselves and our destinies. The truth is that, although we need not be physical slaves of physical masters, we must all be psychophysical slaves of inhuman societal forces unless we can unchain ourselves from unreasonable desires and balance hours of struggle with hours of repose and forgetfulness.

Some desires are unreasonable, and force people to work too hard. Psychiatrists have a special name for these individuals who are never satisfied with their accomplishments. They call them "perfectionists." The term explains itself. These people become irritable and wear themselves out because they will never stop working at a task or stop harping on a problem. They are not satisfied with reasonable accomplishment; they have to "shine" in any situation and do things better than anyone else.

No situation is more fruitful ground for an analytical study of perfectionism and of residual tension in the human organism than an "institution of higher learning." There, individuals who have given many years to academic pursuits are trying to put on the finishing touches with which they hope to gain the pinnacles in their chosen fields of effort. Some will achieve these pinnacles. Others will be left behind because they have inadequacies or lack of balance and common sense. The ones left behind will be the more tense. They have struggled all through their years of schooling, and no one has worried about their tenseness.

Tense pupils throughout our schools follow a very set pattern. In kindergarten they vie with other children for the teacher's favor. In elementary school they struggle for the greatest number of stars on the classroom records. In high school they aim for "straight A," in anticipation of getting into the college of their parents' first choice. In college they permit academic pursuits to narrow their field of vision. They seek not cultural advancement but material and tangible returns. If they chance to get a glimpse of the rewards for those who form close social and personal ties with professors and classmates, as well as achieve training in democratic ways of living through extracurricular responsibilities and participation in athletics, they are left unhappy but unchanged. Finally they feel the need for attending superschools in an effort to get fancy and final degrees.

Fortunately, all students in our graduate schools do not follow this pattern. Degrees are necessary, to be sure, and the highest ones are awarded more readily to those who have learned from associates as well as from books, and who have shown growth in their breadth of view, their judgment, and their regard for the rights of others. They are successfully balanced and therefore secure. Needless to say, there are so few of these true champions that institutions of higher learning are forced to help along individuals of lesser dimensions and give academic degrees to many strugglers whom they know will have indifferent success and actual maladjustments in later life.

It is not the man at the very top who suffers most from hypertension, but the hundreds of less privileged individuals who are struggling toward the pinnacle. The greater burdens of worry, disillusionment, and hypertension are borne by the slightly less gifted in our society, who are permitted to develop strong urges for success and overpowering assurances that they are capable of reaping the highest rewards.

Certain added professional and financial limitations are imposed upon women by custom. It is to be surmised that many women are made more tense because they rebel against the fact that they are not men. It is quite necessary for women to accept their particular roles in business and the professions, and to cease to strive for as high administrative positions and financial success as men. Facing reality will lead to a reduction in tension, while arguing the injustice of such a state of affairs will lead nowhere.

SOCIAL AIMS

While financial returns and recognition for achievements appear to be the focusing aims of many professional and business men and women, social rewards are not to be minimized. "Keeping up with the Jones family" is a social as well as material problem. The appearance one can make, the family one comes from, the behavior of one's relatives all react upon one's happiness. The size of one's body, the quality of one's skin, the color and texture of one's hair have often been determining factors in one's sense of social security. The feeling of shame as the result of one's relatives not being in approved society because of circumstances of birth or because of broken homes is often significant. When these variations from the accepted optimum involve classification with minority or racially "inferior" groups, the barrier to composure and satisfaction is almost insurmountable.

It is easy enough for members of privileged groups to feel slight concern for the injustices which the happenstance of birth imposes, and it is easy for Americans of the "establishment" to rationalize that this land offers everyone a fair and equal chance for economic and social advancement. If such a statement were actually true, there would then be less social unrest. It is to be acknowledged that dissatisfactions in social status have been at the heart of the recent social revolutions all over the world, and to be conjectured that more general education for those who have been deprived, and fair sharing offer the best and surest avenues for social peace.

It is hard to estimate the significance of educational goads, professional urges, business struggles, and social inadequacies in the lives of us all. They are forces against which no one in modern society is immune; but some people withstand them, possibly because they have no physical complaints, possibly because they know how to alternate work with diversion, possibly because they have many friends and loved ones, possibly because they have a satisfying concept of a spiritual force guiding their world and their lives.

NEED FOR PLAY

At least one thing is sure. Tense individuals do not know how to play. Their deep concentration upon worthy goals and their concern for the superficial opinions others hold of them make it impossible for them to be carefree and gay. They have been brought up to believe that work is righteous and that release from serious enterprise is an unworthy escape from responsibility and decorum.

The reason why we are particularly in need of release from work in American society is that overaddiction to business has been considered virtuous. Work, in proper relation and in correct proportion to other aspects of living, is not to be deprecated. But work is not an end of living. It is only a means to an end. Nor is money, which work brings, an end. Nor is what it can buy an end. To live for work and money alone takes the very essence out of life. Work is of value as it makes possible fun and adventure—play. Money is of value as it provides service to others. Work may lead to service to mankind, but when it excludes play it is open to grave criticism. We criticize work not as work, but as a substitute for all other forms of activity. Work is good, but all work and no play makes Jack a very dull and irritating person.

Worth-while recreation must perform two functions: it shall afford lots of fun and jollity, and it shall be creative as well as diverting. The fun and jollity shall not be strained. It shall be much like the play of little children. Those adults who fall into the category of being habitually tense have no illusions, are irritable, and have single-track minds. While their mental horizons are narrow, within this range they are terribly taut and pursue their aims with grim desperation. Psychically they represent a type which is the antithesis of the child. One of the marks of a truly educated man should be that he has not forgotten what childhood should have taught him—to get all the carefree and unacquisitive play possible.

One tragedy resulting from placing work on such a lofty pinnacle is that its adherents often fall so far when they try to escape from it. When these tense individuals are impelled to seek relief from the mental and physical thralldom of work, they are led to the wrong types of "play"—to excesses. When they try to gain relief from the neuromuscular hypertension resulting from work by orgies of other forms of activity, they do the worst thing imaginable. To keep vigorously busy seems to be their only aim. Either they drive themselves with intellectual or manual work, in the time which could provide them leisure, or they keep themselves constantly on the jump from one shallow pastime to another. The channels for a release from work are often as ill chosen as the work itself. In our large urban centers, at least, these channels are often a hectic commercialized whirligig, and excessive use of liquor. Speed, noise, and glitter are the accents of modern amusements, and liquor* is often an escape for many wearied toilers. They escape the virtue of work by being willing to lose control over self.

Let it not be said that we are prudish when we hesitate before accepting liquor as an escape device. Let us take it only when we want it for itself—for its taste or for its food value; but let us not use it as a quick device to escape the sense of frustration that often comes from unrewarding work or the feeling that one is "all tied up in knots."

Recently drugs, like the tranquilizers and LSD, have been used, like liquor, to escape reality and in the hope that they will make life gay and free from care. More will be said about these false sources

---

* Rathbone, Josephine L. *Tobacco, Alcohol and Narcotics.* New York: Oxford Book Company, 1965.

of help. (See Chapter 8.) Let it be said here only that they are used by people who do not have self control and self direction, and do not have resources within themselves to work out their problems.*

HOBBIES

When we seek the creative element in worthwhile recreation we find what have been called hobbies. Many tense people have been urged to find hobbies and many of them have tried, only to become more tense and discouraged. Why? Perhaps they expected too much. The well-adjusted individual is not looking for tangible returns from his hobbies. He knows he will get from them a just return for his labors and nothing more. Prestige cannot help him. Previous accomplishments mean nothing. The final goal may never be reached. Yet he does not care. He is having a good time, and that is all that is important. A tense person cannot gain like benefits from hobbies unless he participates in the same spirit. He must not expect to get from them the same type of returns he gets from work. They are more like play and they must be approached for the same purpose—just for fun. A man needs hobbies to release him from the drudgery of his work, to lighten his load of care, and to bring him into touch with others in an area where he is no more master than they.

Hobbies can be quite serious, but there are no masters screaming "Must" and "Hurry." One can develop a desire to know all there is to be known about some aspect of nature or accomplishment of man, or acquire abilities to actually create with one's own hands as well as with one's own mind. There is no doubt that creative effort focused through special techniques upon self-chosen purposes can be a powerful aid to stability. Toilers whose work gives them little chance for creative thinking should choose to use the mind in leisure time. Those whose work is mainly mental should choose to use the hands and body in the hours available for refreshment.

Books, which help the mind to create new worlds, are wonderful

---

* Kendall, Bruce L. *Clinical Relaxation for Neuroses and Psychoneuroses.* Chapter 6 in *Tension in Medicine* (compiled and edited by Edmund Jacobson), Springfield: Charles C Thomas, 1967.

companions for leisure time; the libraries and bookstalls are brimming with books—books of adventure, books about what great men have thought, books about people who have loved one another. Months and months of leisure time could be spent at home, reading about some phase of history or of current living. In the end one's own life would be immeasurably enriched.

For those who want to make things with their hands, home is as good a haven as it is for those who want to read. There are so many things to do around an apartment or a house—so many gadgets to fix, so many cupboards to tidy, so many garden plots to till. And there can be diverting companionship around a home, for therein live individuals of varying ages. Hours of creative leisure can be especially amusing if they are shared with people of different tastes. What fun to make a wood and paper airplane with a little boy of eight or to hold the yarn for a little lady of eighty! What fun to help the "kids" make molasses candy! What fun for Father to make a chair, a dish, a bookcase in his own shop! What fun for Mother to save five dollars and spend five evenings making a simple dress!

A hobby, to be worth while, usually has some connections with an occupation which has brought income and economic security to someone else. But it need never offer anything more than psychological satisfaction to the person who uses it as a release from the tension of his own remunerative occupation. Furthermore, the hobby must cultivate aesthetic appreciation, to be of most use in freeing a tense person from the bonds which bind him to a dull existence. It is not by chance that most hobbies recommended for hypertense individuals have to do with the arts. In selecting hobbies one would wish to have them beautifying experiences. An artist who paints or sings for his living is not using painting or singing for a hobby. But a civil engineer or a doctor who joins a class in drawing, or a bank clerk who joins a choral society, has chosen painting or singing as a hobby. A woman who collects scraps of lace because they are beautiful or representative of the handiwork of other women is the one with the hobby, not she who makes the lace to sell.

SEARCH FOR BEAUTY

Leisure time affords the only opportunities most people have to go on quests for beauty. Tense people should seek beauty when they snatch a bit of leisure. Beauty is elevating and enriching. Yet beauty cannot be defined. Beauty is in the world about us yet exists only in our appreciation of it. For the appreciation of beauty, we are indebted to our minds as well as to our senses. Special features of shape, color, sound, texture, and movement are perceived by the senses but given meaning by the mind. Yet pictures and songs and all beautiful things defy analysis. Where the sky is blue and the grass is green, where the sea is calm and the breezes blow gently, where the flower is bright and the fruit is ripe, where the child is gay and the mother sings sweetly, there you find beauty. It is by looking for beauty in simple things that one gains the greatest refreshment. Tense people, who need this refreshment, must seek the subtle and unobtrusive beauty of the commonplace. They cannot wait to take a course in aesthetics or until they can retire. They need to look for beauty now.

Strangely enough, through appreciation of beauty comes an enrichment of self that neither a desire to have knowledge nor a desire to do good can ever bring. A very wise teacher, who knew and understood beauty as well as any poet who ever lived—Rabindranath Tagore—sensed this fulfillment of the self as well as this elevation of the emotion through beauty. He expressed the idea something like this: "When art comes, we forget the claims of necessity, the thrift of usefulness; the spires of our temples try to kiss the stars and the notes of our music to fathom the depth of the ineffable."

SECURITY IN LOVE

When we give expression to the emotions, we untie the cords which bind us to the mundane and confining aspects of living. Our energies become focused and our tensions are released. To give expression to feelings of displeasure, anger, and fear may serve as a purge or catharsis, but to give expression to feelings of pleasure and love will serve as an elixir or tonic. In these elevating emotions man has a recourse from pain and discomfort and a release, for his true personality, from the thralldom of struggle and despair.

According to modern psychologists, fundamental impulses are related to self-preservation, self-development, and sex. Any thwarting of these impulses, they say, will lead to a feeling of insecurity, inadequacy, or insignificance, and may lead to personality disorders, of which pathologic worry and melancholy are as common expressions as neurasthenia and irritability. In popular fiction and in current literature in the field of psychiatry, sexual frustration has been given prominence as a cause of emotional and physical breakdowns. If the words "sexual frustration" are changed to the words "lack of friendship and love," the concept is more definitely related to the matter at hand.

"Being in love" usually refers to a relationship between a man and a woman during a particular period in their lives. For this discussion it must take on a more generalized meaning. Probably "loving and being loved in return" serves as a more accurate description of the broader concept. No state of being provides more confidence and power than "being in love," provided the love is reciprocated. It is only unrequited love that leads to depression and a sense of inadequacy.

Loving or being loved, having a friend or being a friend—these emotional satisfactions are more important, in the long run, than anything else in life. Tense people want them more than they want life, yet peaceful love and friendships seem always to be beyond their reach. It is interesting to speculate whether lack of love and friendships has an important share in causing tenseness, or is primarily one of its end results. Everyone knows that the connection is very close. Almost without exception, tense people give evidence of dissatisfactions in their social and personal relationships. If a person has recently begun to show symptoms of hypertension, his condition may even be associated with the immediate loss of a friend or a lover. If a person has built up tension over a long period of time, the counsellor or physician to whom he looks for help will seek in vain for a sympathetic friend or an understanding "helpmate" who has been a source of comfort and companionship in the past.

6

The element in love and affection offering comfort and peace is security. Even in sexual relationships, the quality which makes mating satisfying and enriching is security. It takes more than a bond of marriage, however, to give this security. Before either mate can totally submerge self in union with the other the loved ones must psychologically as well as physically hold each other fast. If the importance of sexual love appears to be minimized in this discussion, it is not because it is not a source of peace in personal lives. Probably the moments of most complete relief from psychological tension are those moments after the culmination of a sexual embrace. These moments are the fragments of ecstasy which poets and philosophers have sung about, but they are not all there is to love.

When one reaches ecstasy in these moments of a love relationship, there is a precious sense of security. Even in less intimate aspects of the state of love, it is also the assurance that one is wanted by the other, is indispensable and therefore secure in the other's love that binds two people together and frees them from struggle and strife, and assures them of comfort and peace. When a love affair ends, it is because one partner no longer needs "security" from the other. On the other hand, when a person finds it difficult to "get over" a love affair, it is because he longs for the security which has been wrenched from him. He may feel chagrin because he was unable to keep his sweetheart's love. He may feel exposed before his other friends as a dupe. He may feel bitter against the fate which tore his lover from him. But more acutely he feels at loose ends with life and drifting without moorings. His insecurity breeds fear of never being wanted again, and worry about a new life scheme. The usual tension which follows the breakdown in a love relationship is born of insecurity.

All other affectional relationships can be described in like manner. The baby "loves" his mother because she gives him security. Her arms enfold him and protect him from harm. She gives him food and keeps him warm. There is no more perfect example of true love than the relationship of mother to child, and child to mother. There is such an interdependence in that relationship that it cannot be said which loves the more. Some will say that the mother gives more, but a mother will say that she gets more. She gets the complete dependence of the other upon herself, and she is enriched thereby. Her every kindness is reciprocated by the longing of the little one for more kindness. All the little one wants is to be wanted and to give himself into the mother's love. All the mother wants is to be wanted, and to be able to succor the little one. Their love is a combination of giving and being wanted.

Anyone who gives selflessly to another, and anyone who establishes a relationship with another so that he is wanted, loves as well as is loved. There is love between older children and their teachers, between boys and girls and their pals, between workers and their "bosses," between patients and their doctors, all because they can do something for each other and because each would be insecure if it were not for the other.

Friendship is like love. We all want as friends those associates who make us feel that they have our interests at heart and will further our life aims. As soon as we doubt the fidelity of those associates to ourselves, as soon as we lose confidence in them, we no longer call them friends. Security in another's regard is the foundation without which there can be no friendship. Without friendships there can be no peace within social relationships.

To be in love, or to have a friend, it becomes necessary to do things for another and to be wanted. This order is not too difficult, and love and friendship are within the reach of everybody. Some people are so blessed by beauty of countenance, by pleasing voice, by gracious manner, that others are always being attracted to them. Why not take a cue from these fortunate ones? Why not acquire an attractive bearing and a well-groomed if not beautiful appearance? Why not work for a more pleasing voice? Why not learn how to be gracious? Why not find a person who needs kindness? Many of the most enriching love affairs and friendships have not come to the beautiful creatures who could not help attracting attention and being wanted, but to less gifted and less selfish people who have learned how to please and to satisfy with kindness. Love and friendship come more from giving than from getting. But the giving cannot be hectic. It must be generous and sincere and tender. There can be no push about it. Calmness, not struggle, breeds confidence.

Do tense people actually lack friends because they are irritable, irascible, and too self-centered, and not because they are unattractive? They are very attractive, many of them, and are appealing to those who are more phlegmatic. As to general appearance, usually, tense individuals can be classed as exceedingly acceptable socially. Some of them are strikingly handsome. Many of them are dynamic and scintillating. They often carry themselves with poise. Perhaps if they were not so self-centered, they would be liked better. Do they fail in their more intimate love relationships because they seek too much for themselves and are too hasty and heedless? Could they make people like them if they would give a little attention to these matters?

In discussing love, everyone can cite numerous examples of discord and disharmony which have wrecked the lives of individuals; but very few observers of socio-political events have analyzed the effect upon social groups of hate and annoyance. It is easy to lose sight of the fact that lack of affection breeds opposition and disharmony between groups as between individuals. In the realm of international affairs, the only way demagogues have been able to get their followers to destroy and maim other peoples has been by impressing upon them how little the other peoples have their interests at heart. In the realm of industry, labor fights back at capital with strikes and propaganda because it feels its interests are not being served by industrial leaders. Labor agitators keep groups of workers stirred up quite effectively by constantly reminding them of how little their "master" cares about their standard of living and their comfort, while he is amassing a fortune which will assure luxury for his own family. The essence of love is selflessness. The essence of hate is selfishness. In international and inter-communal, as well as inter-personal relationships, the one leads to trust and kind dealing, the other to rivalry and fighting.

WORSHIP

If peace is a worthy goal—peace within the individual as well as peace within society—the channels through which it can be achieved are worth studying. When a man's thoughts and deeds take his attention from the dull demands of every day into the realm of the less tangible aspects of living, or into communion with his fellow men, he is approaching an area which may be called spiritual. But tense people do not have broad spiritual horizons. To have a spiritual point of view, one must be capable of detachment from the affairs of the present or immediate future. Tense people, however, find it almost impossible to achieve this essential long-term vision. Because they are so dissatisfied with the present, they can conceive of no ultimate good uncontrolled by themselves. They appear to believe that the only rewards life has to offer must be wrested from her. They acknowledge no force greater than petty man; and, because of their arrogance and trust in material values, they have no trust in spiritual forces.

This lack of spiritual security may be the most fundamental psychological characteristic of tense individuals. It may be the most significant aspect, also, of present-day "Western" culture. It may be the very reason why the need to relax is so universal among men and women in American society today. Furthermore, if the individual seeking release from tension has tried numerous other devices to help him to relax, he may still be unchanged unless he can gain a fresh point of view toward ultimate essentials. Without faith in a greater force than man, without faith in love between men, the individual is forced to feel unprotected and starkly alone.

When one is distraught and tense it seems to be particularly difficult to find "a greater force" to worship. Perhaps it is because tense people struggle too hard. Perhaps they are too wrapped up in their own petty problems to envision any large pattern for living, in which the individual can be relieved from struggle. Even organized religions offer too little help. One world religion—Judaism—has within it seeds of constant struggle because its followers believe they are the chosen of God. Another religion—Mohammedanism—has had one period of world conquest to destroy all "non-believers." Another religion—Christianity—has gotten very far from the simple creed of its selfless founder.

The founders of all the great formalized religions of the world were closer in their concept of righteousness than are their followers of today. Their followers have encased their teachings in ritual and pomp. They have created cathedrals of worship and have bickered over items leading to sectarianism, but have not obeyed the essential and simple dictates of the wise philosophers whom they profess to follow. They are selfish, and desire material rewards more than spiritual peace. Yet, many wise young people all over the world, in every religious sect, are struggling to find a satisfying, non-destroying faith. Faith they must have. Religions are quests to find faiths, to find explanations for such problems as whence we—our souls—came, what forces are directing our destinies, and whither we—our souls—are going. Tense people need these faiths.

OFFSETTING PSYCHOLOGICAL CAUSES OF TENSION

Lack of satisfaction from work, lack of joy, lack of friends and loved ones, lack of faith are the sources of insecurity. The fears and worries of tense individuals stem from these sources as well as from their self-centeredness. In order to escape, they are compelled toward various forms of over-exertion.

Just as the previous chapter, in its discussion of the more physical causes of fatigue and tension, ended with a discussion of hyperactivity and refusal to take enough rest as the most important aspect of the syndrome, so this chapter, with its emphasis upon the more psychological causes, must end on the same note. It is necessary to offset the hyperactivity which results from insecurity and which is responsible for more hypertension and subsequent breakdown. No matter what the psychological causes of over-effort may be, it is the resulting increase in physical neuromuscular activity which is the acute problem to be overcome in all cases of residual hypertonus.

It is not to be expected that individuals for whom work, play, love, and worship offer many conflicts will be able to experience continuous peace. But they may learn how to balance rest against effort, calmness against strain, quiet against turmoil. If they can keep themselves in psychophysical health, they can acquire skills which will offset the tensions of living and prevent cumulative fatigue. In psychophysical terms, they can achieve some degree of peace if they can offset hypertension in their personal relationships. Each individual will find a slightly different set of factors to explain his own situation. It is hoped that this chapter will afford enough ideas to help every reasonable person untangle some of the taut threads in his own life.

5

The More Physical Methods of Treatment

A SENSIBLE PROGRAM

THE PERSON WHO IS WELL and has nothing to worry about, who works consistently but without over-effort, who has sense enough to rest when he becomes tired, will never have to learn special techniques for relaxing. But how rare is that person! Even the most composed and well balanced of us cannot answer to that description at all times. This chapter is written for those who may be over-burdened and who may be in need, temporarily, of aids to repose, as well as for the unfortunate person who is continuously showing signs of tenseness. In some respects this chapter ties together many of the ideas advanced in the preceding chapters, but it also offers specific suggestions which tend to make it more practical than the others.

These pages are not written for the individual who is suffering from false fatigue or from "feelings of fatigue." Instead, they aim to reach the hard worker and heavy worrier who is actually distressed to a degree that can be measured by nervous indigestion, by sleeplessness, by pain in the neck, by rapid heart, or by any of the other physical or psychological symptoms of residual neuromuscular hypertonus which are included in Selye's concept of stress. (See p. 5.) They may be of much less interest to the continuously healthy, happy person who gets tired periodically but who knows how to get rested again.

The normal "good and tired" feeling that comes at the end of a purposeful and satisfying day is not called "fatigue," nor complained of, by most of us. It has too pleasant a tang and is too easily dispelled by simple diversion, nourishment, and sleep. Nor is it necessary to suggest special techniques in relaxation for such a condition. Such techniques are needed for the chronic discomfort that makes it impossible for the sufferer to enjoy his food or fall asleep at will. It is with this chronic and abnormal fatigue, including its phase of hypertension, that this chapter is concerned. Chronic fatigue does not come suddenly. It has been accumulating for days, months, and years. It may take a long time to dispel. The dispelling will demand a high degree of determination and cooperation and discipline from the person who is trying to learn to relax. Yet success is sure to reward him if he has no organic disturbance, and if he can become master of himself emotionally.

Many of the most important techniques for the release of tension demand long-term planning, and their results are to be recognized only after months of effort. They are intangible and consist of psychophysical aids to general improvement in health, of more wholesome diversion and recreation, of a more sensible rhythm between work, diversion, and rest, of less hurry and struggle toward unimportant goals, of a reduction in self-centeredness and self-seeking, and of an increase in spiritual resources. (Refer to Chapters 4 and 6.)

SPECIFIC TECHNIQUES

There are techniques, however, which are tangible and can be used specifically to release neuromuscular tensions in local areas of the body—the arms, the legs, the trunk, the face. It is possible to reduce tension and bring about relaxation by rhythmic exercises for the extremities and the trunk; by devices to encourage greater flexibility in all the joints, but particularly in those of the spine and chest, thereby facilitating better functioning of the diaphragm; and by concentrating the attention upon reducing tonic contraction in localized muscles. Some of these techniques have been arrived at empirically. Others have been selected because they stand up to the test of scientific measurement. All of them are worth trying, however, if one wishes to counteract the causes of residual muscular tension, of discomfort, and of dysfunction discussed in previous chapters.

Rhythmic exercises, particularly for the spine, will improve circulation and free muscles from holding parts of the body statically. Increased flexibility will demand release of tension in the small muscles which support joints and tend to restrict movements. Better functioning of the diaphragm will improve the circulation. Attention to the reduction of residual tonus in any muscles will react upon the whole organism by cutting down on the bombardment of the central nervous system by sensory messages from the muscle sheaths. (See p. 40.) Relaxation is thus attained.

These techniques for the release of tension demand hours of practice. This part of the discussion relates not to a change in point of view nor to a change in behavior, which can be brought about by an order to the cook or a visit to a physician or by a series of vacations. Just a decision to modify the pace of one's life will not automatically release tautness in the muscles which have become overtense. Release of tautness must be practiced. The following suggestions for this release are not difficult, but they call for repeated periods of practice which will consume some time each day until the ability to relax at will has been surely acquired. The rewards in greater comfort and greater energy, however, will be compensation enough for the time spent.

RHYTHMIC EXERCISES

Any teacher of gymnastics or any leader of folk and interpretative dances can outline a scheme of rhythmic exercises for the arms and legs and the trunk. The exercises suggested below have been selected from a long list because they have proved successful with very tense subjects.* They are extremely simple and almost "foolproof." No one can harm himself in doing any of them; and they can be repeated over and over again, with benefit, without danger of mus-

* Rathbone, Josephine L. and Hunt, Valerie V. *Corrective Physical Education* (7th Ed.), selections from Chapter 6. Philadelphia, W. B. Saunders Co., 1965.

cular strain. It is to be recommended that at least one exercise for the arms, one for the legs, and one for the trunk be used in each practice period.

The following free and loose swinging movements are suggested for the *arms:*

1. Kneeling, sitting on a low stool, or standing in erect position, swing both arms forward and then sideward letting them drop during the swings so that the hands brush the thighs on each motion. An effort should be made to keep the shoulders low. Do not hurry, and continue for half a minute or more.

2. Kneeling, sitting on a low stool, or standing in erect position, swing both arms from a position with forearms crossed in front of the chest to an attitude with the arms extended in oblique position above and behind the head. Keep the arms moving rhythmically, for several rounds, through the entire arc of motion in the suggested directions.

3. Sitting on the edge of a chair with one overhanging hand clenched very tightly, swing that arm forcibly in large circles, the right clockwise and the left counterclockwise. Feel as though you are swinging it out of its socket. Be sure to keep the hand clenched.

The following exercises, suggested for the *legs,* are to be done in the same free swinging style:

1. Sitting on the edge of a table, with the lower legs hanging free, let the legs swing alternately forward and backward. Keep them moving alternately in rhythm to a simple tune like "Yankee Doodle." This motion will free tautness in the thighs and improve circulation in the knees and lower legs.

2. Sitting on the edge of a table, with the lower legs hanging free, swing both legs from side to side in unison. The lower legs will remain parallel. This motion will free tautness in the region of the hip joints.

3. Standing with one side close to a table so that the hand on that side may give support, swing the opposite or outside leg forward and backward loosely from the hip joint. This exercise should be performed in the stocking feet or in very sensible low-heeled shoes.

The following exercises are suggested for the *trunk:*

1. Assuming a position on all fours with knees separated a few

inches, with thighs perpendicular to the floor, with the shoulders the same height as the hips and the elbows bent slightly, hump the back and let the head hang down; then extend the spine with the head held high. Emphasis should be placed on humping or flexing in the lumbar region and lowering or extending in the thoracic region of the spine. To make this movement a little more difficult, but much more effective for freeing the spinal muscles from the tautness that develops when the trunk is held erect, let the elbows bend and the trunk swing backward when the head is up and the chest is low. Then let the trunk move forward and the arms extend again as the head droops and the back humps.

2. Let the body roll loosely. The subject should lie on his back, on the floor, with his hands over his head. He will roll over onto his face by letting the lead come from the hip away from the direction in which the body is to move. The shoulders, head, hand and feet will drag behind until they are drawn over by the weight of the body. From the face-lying position, the body will continue to move in the same direction, being drawn over by the lead of the "back" shoulder. It is well to continue this loose rolling for several turns, before reversing. The body may be permitted to rest for a few seconds in any position it assumes after a few turns.

3. Kneeling with the feet under the hips and the hands reaching over the head, let the trunk sway and twist so that the hands can transcribe half circles on the floor followed by half circles in the opposite direction in the air. The movements should be full and sweeping, with the trunk moving an equal number of times, in both directions.

4. Standing with hips supported against the wall, the feet apart and a few inches from the wall, the trunk bent forward and the arms drooping, let the body sway in a semicircle from side to side with arms and head loose.

5. Standing with the hips supported against the wall, in the same manner as in the previous exercise, let the trunk make a great circle. The trunk should sway to one side, swing across to the opposite side, and be raised with the lateral trunk muscles before dropping down to the starting position. The arms will transcribe an arc in the air from one side to the other, up over the head, and down to the side from which the movement started.

EXERCISES TO INCREASE FLEXIBILITY IN JOINTS

Several of the above exercises will help to increase flexibility in the joints, although their main purposes are to set rhythmic motions for untensing opposing muscles and to assist circulation. When it comes actually to increasing flexibility, a distinction is made between rapid motions of a swinging character, and positions which demand precise stretching of joint structures at the limit of motions. The latter are the more effective.

Movements which encourage flexibility and positions which tend to stretch joint structures mildly have not been used in modern "corrective physical education" as much as their worth recommends. Too much attention has been placed upon the building up of tonus in muscles, to make it easier for the subject to maintain certain socially approved postures in standing and sitting. Efforts have centered upon held positions, the principle involved being that every attitude or posture adopted is associated with a rush of sensory stimuli into the central nervous system; so that every time this acceptable posture is assumed, its more frequent adoption is facilitated. If this type of practice is carried too far, however, fatigue results. As was noted in Chapters 2 and 3, much of the hypertonus which leads toward discomfort and overfatigue comes from just such posturing in attitudes of attention and in postures associated with work, even mental work. As important as it may be, under certain circumstances, to build up an efficient degree of tonus for strength or appearance, it becomes quite unnecessary to suggest exercises for that purpose in a chapter on techniques in relaxation. Exercises to increase flexibility in joints and not rigidity are more in order.

The following suggestions come from my clinical and laboratory experience. It gave great satisfaction, however, to learn that no less a medical and psychiatric authority than Abraham Myerson advocated that his "tense" patients move the segments of their bodies through their full ranges of motion at least once every day.

A region of the body which frequently needs to be freed of tension is the neck, but since rhythmic swingings of the head would lead to dizziness, in most instances, it is necessary to perform all motions of the head quite slowly and to aim particularly at increasing the flexibility in joints of the neck.   Here is an opportunity for an example of a very simple type of exercise, the immediate purpose of which is to increase flexibility in joints, but the ultimate results of which are to free muscles of extra tension, to improve circulation, and to relieve discomfort.

Sitting with the spine erect and the shoulders low, turn the head and twist and bend the neck so that the chin touches one collarbone. Do not move the shoulders.   If the chin will not reach the collarbone, let the neck remain in the uncomfortable position of forced twist for a few seconds.   The hand on the side to which the head is inclined can be placed over the head to add a little weight as a stretching force.   Never force or jerk the part, for that type of motion will only encourage muscle tissue to contract.   When muscle tissue is stretched suddenly, it reflexly contracts.   Stretching must be maintained for twenty or thirty seconds to be effective.   (See p. 41.)

The following exercises for other regions of the body incorporate the same principle of maintained stretch of soft tissues to make possible an increase in joint flexibility:

1. Lie on the back with an extension roll under the back where the bulge of the curve is greatest or where, for any reason, it is desirable to increase extension.   The roll may be made of a bath towel or a large magazine.   If the structures in front of the shoulder joints are tight, the arms should be bent slightly and placed so that the backs of the hands and the elbows rest on the floor.   This position may be impossible at first, but it can be acquired, eventually, if there is no structural defect in the shoulder joints or arms.   At first it may be desirable to put weights about as heavy as medium-sized books on the wrists, to hold the arms down.   This position should be maintained for only two to three minutes, on the first day.   The time should be extended at subsequent practice periods.

2. Sitting on the floor with the legs crossed in "Turkish fashion," press the knees toward the floor by steady pressure from the hands. The same principle of maintained position with gradual stretch of tight structures, described above, should be followed in this position for the hip joints.

3. Lying on the back with the knees held close together and raised to the chest while the arms lie with back of the hands on the

floor, as in exercise 1 above, roll the lower limbs so that the outer surface of one thigh touches or approximates the floor. Do not let the legs unflex. After a few seconds twist the trunk and roll the lower limbs to the other side, in this way giving the spine a good twisting.

4. Lying on the back with the arms stretched sideward raise one leg straight in the air, lower it toward the opposite hand, and let it remain in that position for half a minute or more before returning it to the starting position. Repeat with the other leg. This is not a rhythmic movement; the positions are to be held. Because of twisting of the trunk and because of the weight of the leg alone acting as a stretching force on the structures of the lower back, this exercise lends itself to the freeing from tension of those structures without danger of wrenching.

5. Standing with hips against the wall, feet 4 inches away from the wall and 18 inches apart, bend the trunk forward with arms and head loose and all the weight hanging loosely from the sacrum and lower back. (If the person has had some back strain which has resulted in pain, and if there is a tendency for the muscles of the lower back to contract reflexly because of the pain, it is well to swing the trunk around to either side before rising, in order to raise the trunk by the contraction of the muscles on the other side of the trunk.)

6. Sitting on one hip with legs bent and feet placed at the opposite side, the arm on that side bent so that the clenched fist can press against the side of the chest wall, and the other arm placed in a curve over the head, push the chest cage toward the side of the raised arm with forcible stretching of that side. This exercise will stretch the lateral structures of the trunk particularly.

7. Standing with one foot raised on a chair, bend the trunk forward, making an effort to place the head on the knee. This position will stretch the structures behind the thigh as well as along the back.

It will be appropriate at this place to discuss briefly a whole system of exercise which has been built up on maintained positions, not on movements. It is the system of Hatha Yoga, which scholars and scientists in India are trying to revive. The following suggestions come from the teachings of Swami Kuvalayānanda of Bombay, with whom I studied long before the fad of Yoga had become popular. I went to India to study Hatha Yoga in the late nineteen thirties. (See pp. 150 and 154.)

Hatha Yoga is "that system of Yoga which starts with the purification of the body as the first step toward spiritual perfection." The aim of Yoga on the physical side is to avoid disease and ensure health by establishing and maintaining physiological harmony in the human body.

The physical exercises are called *âsanas*. They are really held positions or poses, and a discussion of some of them fits neatly into our consideration of exercises to improve flexibility of the body. Âsanas are divided into two principal groups: cultural and meditative. The cultural âsanas, or poses, according to Yogic scholars, are practiced for training the circulatory, nervous, and endocrine systems, whereas the meditative poses are assumed in order to eliminate physiological disturbances resulting from mental activity. Our interest at this point is concentrated upon a few of the âsanas used for body culture. In Yogic practice there are never any jerking movements. What little bend is possible in any of these âsanas should first be secured and maintained for some time before a greater bend is attempted.

1. An âsana which helps to stretch all the posterior structures of the body has been called the "plough pose," because in this position the body imitates the shape of the Indian plough. The plough pose helps to keep the spinal column fully flexible. When we remember that real youth is invariably characterized by a flexible spine, and old age always renders the spine more rigid, one can understand why such exercises are of value.

In assuming the "plough pose," the subject lies on his back, with his arms at his sides. Then he slowly raises his legs, keeping them straight and curling the spine up to follow them, until the toes touch the floor beyond the head. The knees should be kept straight, fully stretching the hamstrings. If it is impossible to touch the toes to the floor on the first try, a chair may be placed beyond the head, and the feet placed on its seat. Never should there be any forced straining. Little by little, with successive attempts, the feet can be lowered until the toes do touch the floor. Positions gained should be held for a few seconds each time. Ultimately, the position of the feet can be adjusted farther and farther away from the head to put the maximum pressure on the lumbosacral region, on the lower thoracic region, or on the upper thoracic region of the spine. Finally the hands can be removed from their original positions and locked above the head, while the toes are pushed farther away from the head so that pressure is experienced at the cervical part of the spine. These more difficult phases of the plough pose should be attempted only after the previous ones become easy.

2. An âsana which reverses the curve of the spine has been called the "cobra pose" because it gives one the appearance of a hooded snake under irritation. The subject lies prone, with his forehead touching the floor, and with his hands placed at either side of his chest.

The student then raises his head and bends the neck backward as far as possible, completely throwing out his chin. During this attempt his chest is kept close to the ground, the trunk, so to say, taking no part in the movement. When the head is fully swung backward, the student begins to work the deep muscles of his back. By their contraction he slowly raises his chest. When the student is only a beginner, he supports his rising thorax with his hands, gradually increasing the angle between his arm and forearm. But, as he becomes accustomed to this practice, he tries to depend upon the muscles of the back alone for raising his chest; and, though the hands are allowed to work as previously, comparatively little burden is now put upon them.

After maintaining the pose for the prescribed time, the student begins to efface the spinal curve and bring down his chest. Here, too, he proceeds gradually in his work. First, the lumbar curve is obliterated, each vertebra being relieved of its pressure which now travels upward. The thoracic and cervical curves are effaced in the same way, till the whole *trunk* lies in a horizontal *plane* and the forehead touches the ground as it did originally.

3. A twisted pose has been selected from Yogic sources. It may be described as follows:

To start with, the student sits on the floor with his legs fully stretched out and placed close to each other. He then bends one of his legs at the knee, say the right; and, turning it outward so that the outside of the thigh rests on the floor, sets its heel tight on the perineum. Sometimes an attempt is made to sit on the heel, but this is a wrong procedure and should be studiously avoided. When properly adjusted the right sole will closely touch the left thigh. Then the student withdraws his left leg and, bending it in the knee, arranges it in such a way that the left foot rests on the right side of the right thigh.

The main feature of the pose consists in twisting the spinal column. The steps taken up to now are only a preparation for securing this twist with mechanical advantage derived from particular arrangements of the limbs. The erect knee, here the left, is now to be used as a fulcrum upon which the right shoulder-joint is to rest its back. This is done by passing the right hand round the left knee and rotating the whole trunk to the left, till the right shoulder and the left knee are pressing against each other. With a view to obtaining a full rotation of the trunk and preventing the knee from slipping off the shoulder, the right hand is fully stretched out and made to grasp the left foot or its toes which is now available on the opposite side. Care should be taken not to strain the elbow joint. This danger is avoided by firmly setting the shoulder against the knee.

In order to obtain additional mechanical advantage for securing the spinal twist, the student now employs the left hand. He swings it back and tries to have a hold upon the right thigh just below the groin. Thus there are two forces operating upon the trunk, twisting it to the left; and these two together are competent to effect the fullest possible twist. The contortion, however, does not affect the cervical vertebrae. In order that these might cooperate with the remaining vertebrae, the head is swung to the extreme left till the chin is almost in a line with the left shoulder. Throughout the practice, the student takes care to see that his chest stands erect and does not droop down. The same pose is to be tried using the left extremities instead of the right and vice versa so that the two opposite twists would move between them the different vertebrae through all the rotation possible.

Some American critics of this book will say that these Yogic âsanas do not warrant the space devoted to them. Some Indian critics will say that the descriptions are too brief, and that other

7

advantages than the one of increasing flexibility in joints should have been stressed, and, also, more âsanas described. To both sets of critics the answer is the same. In this book certain principles have been set down upon which to base a broad program for the release of neuromuscular hypertonus. Whenever we discover techniques that advance these principles in practice we should accept them, and weave them into the fabric of a corrective program divorced from any particular system.

Although we recognize in these Yogic practices certain techniques which may be used with benefit in a program for keeping fit in the United States, we are fully aware of the fact that nowhere in America is there a physical, psychological, and cultural environment where Hatha Yoga, as a system of exercise, can be used to full advantage. The âsanas selected for description in the previous pages are to be recommended as any exercises may be for specific therapeutic results. They do not constitute the Yogic system, nor would I wish to advocate such a system for general adoption in the United States.

EXERCISES TO RELEASE TENSION IN THE BREATHING MECHANISM

Relaxation of the diaphragm is particularly desirable for subjects who are too tense. Every single case which has been referred to me for techniques in relaxation has exhibited restrictions in breathing, and residual hypertonus in the diaphragm. If the subject has worked too hard, he has held his breath; if he has been afraid, he has caught his breath; if he has been ill and inactive, he has not used much breath. Either the diaphragm has not contracted enough or it has not relaxed enough. It has lost elasticity, as it were, and moves through a very narrow span. To make it contract to as flat a shape as possible and to relax into as high a dome as possible must be one of the first aims of a program designed to help a person to fully relax.

Some of the techniques to help the diaphragm to relax, recommended below, are taken from the same source as the first exercises listed above. Let us describe just a few which have proved effective.

1. Lying on the back with knees bent and feet resting on the floor, take a deep breath, permitting both the abdominal wall and the chest to rise; then let the air out through the mouth with a gasp. Repeat four or five times at irregular intervals. Be very sure to have the knees raised, in order to take stretch away from the abdominal muscles.

2. Lying on the back with knees bent and feet resting on the floor, change the thoracic and abdominal pressure by first inhaling and filling the upper part of the chest, then forcing the pressure against the diaphragm, pushing the abdomen out, followed by retracting the abdomen while enlarging the upper part of the chest, inhaling more if desired; and finally exhaling completely through the mouth with a short gasp. This exercise can be performed only a few times, if done properly, without inducing dizziness. It should be done less than ten times in series.

3. Lying on the back with the knees bent, or sitting "Turkish fashion" with the spine erect, control the breathing. In the Yogic system there are many exercises of inhaling and exhaling. They are called pranayamas, and were devised to put breathing under control of the will. Obvious results are physiologic, but more subtle and possibly more important results are psychologic. Not only does the counting, which must accompany these techniques, take the mind off all else; but the entailed escape from worries and the resulting disappearance of unpleasant sensations bring quietness and repose.

Perhaps only one pranayama, which can be modified in many ways, is enough for those who study this book. It will increase range of flexibility of the chest, with resulting effects on the circulation and intermittent pressure on the abdominal viscera. It will induce fuller relaxation of the diaphragm, so that breath is not held as in states of anxiety and fear. It will give the patient awareness of being able to control himself: to stop the sensation of his heart "fluttering," to relieve the "butterflies" in his stomach, and to ease his backache. If he falls to sleep doing this exercise, he feels rewarded, and all because he did something for himself, not because he took some medicine or depended on someone else.

Let us start this pranayama in the back lying position, with a pillow under the knees to allow the thighs to roll outward, and with the arms in any comfortable position without pressing on the body. Let us set a rhythm of one count to each heartbeat when one is resting. After this rhythm is learned, there is no need to attend to the pulse. Let us start by inhaling for four counts and exhaling for four counts. There should be no straining in either phase, but the motion should be complete in the time allowed. Particularly should the exhaling be maximal in the four counts allowed. Gradually the chest excursion will become greater. If there is an involuntary and unusually large inhalation, the exercise is to be stopped and a fresh routine started after a brief period. If it seems as though it would be better to set a rhythm of six counts for inhalation and six counts for exhalation, that can be done, but then there will be only six or seven breaths each minute. In therapeutic practice there is no advantage in reducing the breathing cycles to fewer than six or four per minute. A full expiration is what is really being aimed at, with maximum relaxation of the diaphragm. The proportion of time between inspiration and expiration may be modified. Sometimes it will be fun to allow twice as long for the expiration as for the inspiration. At other times one can count six for inhaling, four for holding, six for exhaling, and four for holding before starting the cycle over again. Any variation which proves entertaining may be tried.

A patient should set a time aside, each day, to practice pranayamas, just as a person should set a regular time aside to practice any skill. A good time is ten or fifteen minutes before lunch and again before dinner. In most places of business there are rest rooms for men and women, with cots, where an employee can be free from interruptions for brief periods of time. Executives, who are particularly in need of help in relaxing, can arrange for retiring rooms even if they are in closets, behind filing cabinets. At home, before meals, there should be no interruptions. Telephones can be taken off of hooks for ten to fifteen minutes at a time, and anyone in need of help can be protected from interruptions by other members of the family.

TRAINING OF MUSCLES TO RELAX AT WILL

When we wish to train the muscles to relax at will, it becomes necessary to place the subject in a position in which no muscle tonus is needed. A prolonged vertical position is extremely fatiguing, as everyone knows, and is a potential source of irritability and discomfort. The best way to dispel the tensions resulting from the maintenance of an erect posture is to let the body assume the horizontal plane. If total recumbency is impossible, some comfort can be gained in the sitting posture if the head can be lain back on a firm support or forward on arms folded across a desk or table. These attitudes will at least rest the neck muscles. If the legs can be raised, as the head and upper trunk are tilted backward, and if the arms can be supported, the total effect may be quite satisfying.

When all is said and done, the best rest position is reclining on the back on a firm bed or couch. It may be more comfortable to have the neck supported by a firm roll and the lower back supported by a small, firm cushion. If desirable, the knees can be raised slightly on other rolls or cushions. The thighs should rotate outward, and the arms should not be pressed close to the body. The arms may be at the sides in the half-bent and rolled-out attitude of an infant as he sleeps on his back. In total recumbency, with the arms and legs supported thus in slight flexion, it is possible to get maximum relaxation of muscles without ligamentous strain. This position is more refreshing, always, than any other.

If a person argues in favor of a distorted position on the abdomen and side of the face, it is because he has found comfort from pressure on his ventral surface. Perhaps the sense of well-being comes from surface pressure alone. Before a baby comes into this world there is pressure on that surface, and it remains for him an erotic zone. Perhaps the sense of well-being comes from pressure within the viscera. When an abdominal wall has lost its tonus, permitting organs to be dragged down by gravity, while the trunk is vertical, circulation in these organs is disturbed. Opportunity for these organs to come back to more "normal" position and to be held pressed together will affect the circulation and lead to a sense of well-being. Yet, if one lies too long on the abdomen, the spine and neck will be twisted. Therefore a symmetrical position on the back will prove to be the best one in which to practice conscious relaxation.

THE JACOBSON TECHNIQUE

Through the ages, a number of practitioners have postulated systems for relaxing various regions of the body. No suggestions are more helpful than those of Edmund Jacobson, a Chicago physician who spent many years on a technique which has proved most satisfactory for even difficult cases. It is a technique, also, which can be subjected to scientific appraisal.* As Dr. Jacobson stated in a letter to me, the chief interest of his clinic has been the development of methods which can be measured scientifically. He further added that the significant technique is the removal of the last remnants of tension. The work was on "residual tensions" or "basic tensions"; therefore his techniques are of unique interest.

The Jacobson technique demands great determination and cooperation on the part of the subject, and depends upon the subject alone. The subject does not have to put his faith in anyone else, nor learn any complicated routine. Under the observation of a helper, at first, the subject contracts certain isolated muscles and muscle groups until he is sure that he recognizes tension. Then he is instructed to "go in the negative direction." Whatever it is that he does or does not do when he begins to relax, that he is to continue on and on, past the point where the part seems to him perfectly relaxed.

* Jacobson, Edmund. *Progressive Relaxation*. The University of Chicago Press, Chicago, Rev. ed., 1938. (Original and most complete description of theory and methodology.)
A very important aspect of treatment, described in *Progressive Relaxation*, is the cultivation of the muscle sense. Although, in persistent cases of residual hypertonus, it is necessary to acquire the sense of muscle tension, in less extreme cases of nervousness, where opportunity is lacking to give thorough nervous reeducation, the cultivation of the muscle sense may be omitted. Jacobson is willing to be quoted as saying that it is possible to give a fairly adequate course in relaxation training without recourse to the development of the muscle sense. For a book of this kind, to be used by pupils and patients who are anxious to pursue the most exacting techniques, if less intensive ones fail to bring results, it is valuable to emphasize the mechanism of cultivating the muscle sense.

When the subject is practicing by himself, he is not to contract before relaxing, but is to begin at the stage in which he happens to be. The subject learns to localize tensions wherever they occur during nervous irritability and excitement and to relax them away. It has been demonstrated in actual practice that the residual hypertonus in any and all regions of the body can be reduced by localized ("differential") or generalized ("progressive") conscious relaxation.

During the first lessons, in conscious releasing of muscular tension, it is desirable to concentrate the attention mainly upon the arms with their shoulder regions, and the legs with their hip joint regions. As skill in releasing tension in these areas increases, total relaxation will become easier. Finally, however, it is necessary to learn how to release residual tonus consciously in the muscles of the chest, in the back and neck, and ultimately in the face. Only when the muscles of the speech mechanism and the forehead and eyes are free from excess tension can one be said to be totally relaxed. When that stage is reached repose is complete.

Dr. Jacobson has been kind enough to permit his own words to be used in describing his technique. Let us turn the discussions over to him and get help directly from him.

For your first session,* "you are to close your eyes and to lie as much at rest as you know how for a few minutes, after which Doctor will begin with you. When you cross your legs, he instructs you not to do so, without explaining why."

Relaxing the Arms

"After a little interval, following his directions, you raise your right arm vertically, holding it up stiffly, while at the same time you clench your fist. . . . Now, cease to do that, letting the fingers go. If you do this properly, the fingers will uncurl, but not completely, while the arm will fall by its own weight. That was a little better, but not much. Let it rest for a few minutes. No! you are opening your eyes: keep them closed throughout. There go your legs again: do not cross them.

* Jacobson, Edmund. *You Can Sleep Well*. New York, Whittlesey House, McGraw-Hill Book Company, Inc., 1938. pp. 76–130. Quoted with permission of publisher.

"Once more, raise your arm, clench your fist and observe that this is your doing. Let the arm fall limply. That is better. Note what is meant by relaxing: it is simply *the negative of doing.*

"Begin again, this time without moving your arm from your side; hold it there stiffly like a rod, so that it would not easily bend at the elbow, but also clench your fist. Do this in stages, gradually, taking a minute or more to stiffen it to the utmost. That is correct. Hold it so. Your arm lies quietly, but it is stiff, not relaxed. This shows you clearly that lying still is not necessarily the same as lying relaxed. A part or the whole of you may be still, but rigid; only when it is both still and limp is it relaxed.

"Continue to hold your arm stiffly at your side for another minute more. Not quite so stiffly. Still a little less. Very well, but continue on, still a little less. That is what you do when you relax; or rather, what you do *not* do. Continue that further until you are not bothering to do anything at all with your arm or fingers. On and on, past that point, for your arm is still ever so slightly stiff, although you do not know it. What is that called? You mean the tension left after you lie down but fail to relax completely? That is 'residual tension.'

"Try it again. Stiffen your right arm as before, without bending it but making all the muscles feel firm to the touch of your left fingers. Do it gradually, hold it for a minute, then let go gradually, using several minutes more. No! you let go too abruptly. Do so more slowly, in order to give yourself the opportunity to comprehend the diminishing action in your arm. Good! That is relaxing gradually. Sometimes it is better to relax suddenly.

"Rest for several minutes with the right arm relaxed. Repeat the tension again. Three times in all are sufficient. Spend the following forty minutes in rest, with the right arm relaxed, as your model. . . . You are to lie quietly, not even stiffening your right arm. If, almost as if unbeknown to you, it becomes stiff at any moment or moves inadvertently, you are to recognize the fact and remedy it at once. You are to cease being stiff, yet not to move. This will mean that you will not bother to do anything at all with that arm. . . .

"Relaxation gives no feeling of numbness; it is a simple negative
. . . an absence of feeling. This negativeness, so to speak, seems in a
sense to include a greater part of your body. It is the best rest you
have had in a long time. Reluctantly you arise when the Doctor
tells you that the hour period is over. You gladly accept his invita-
tion to call again."

The following are instruction sheets prepared for a subject by
Dr. Jacobson:

PRACTICE PERIOD 1

"Position:	On back, with eyelids closed, legs not crossed.
Length of period:	Thirty minutes, if you are restless. Fifty min-utes, if you lie without marked discomfort.
Tension:	Raise right arm and clench fist. Note, as you do so, the feeling of activity throughout the entire arm.
Relaxation:	Let the arm fall limply, while the fingers partly uncurl. Do not shift the arm after it falls, however slightly. Do not hold it stiffly quiet. Rest is continued for several minutes.

"Repeat the tension and relaxation as above described two more
times. Devote the remainder of period (about twenty to forty
minutes) to rest alone, with no more tensions.

PRACTICE PERIOD 2

"Repeat with both arms what you did in Practice Period 1 with
the right arm alone.

"During rest periods, relax both arms at your side, without shifts
and without holding yourself rigid.

PRACTICE PERIOD 3

"Lie on your back with eyes closed in a position which seems restful. Omit tensions. Relax from the outset. Make it your goal not
to move at all during the entire period. If you fall short of this
goal, at least reduce the number of movements to a minimum.

Caution: *Do not hold* any part quiet; for this is being rigid,
                    not relaxed.

Purpose of this   Tensing at the outset of a period is a way to
period: learn to relax, but is to be discontinued gradu-
                    ally as you learn to become relaxed without
                    this device. The purpose of this period is to try
                    to make the relaxation automatic and to avoid
                    associating it with preliminary tension."

Relaxing the Legs

The next time you come for instruction you will resume your
former position on the couch and close your eyes, as Dr. Jacobson
directs, for a brief rest.

"Again you lie on your back, with legs at full length. In the
course of five or ten minutes, he directs you to bend down both feet
and the toes as well. You are to stretch down the toes to the utmost
and hold them so for several minutes without bending at the knees.
While you do so, he calls on you to notice that you are actively doing
something in your legs. This time you are less engrossed in your
personal problems than you were on the first evening with the
Doctor and you believe that you catch a little more clearly his intent
in having you notice the activity in your legs. Gradually, following
his directions, you cease to stretch your legs and to bend down your
feet and toes quite so much, then a little less, and a little less, taking
one or two minutes for your feet and toes to become completely limp
at the joints. He requires you to repeat the bending and unbending
several times; but allows an interval of several minutes for complete
relaxation between each unbending and the following act. When,
during this interval, you open your eyes and begin to speak, he cor-
rects you at once. No more does he permit you to shift your position

or to move even a finger without comment. He has requested you to relax your arms along with your legs.

"During the following forty minutes neither of you speaks a word. He sits by quietly and does nothing to disturb you for the most part. An exception occurs after a lapse of about twenty minutes. You were not feeling quite comfortable. In fact, you were wondering whether you might not shift your legs, particularly the right one. Indeed, although you had not noticed it, you had a little while previously moved both elbows just a little. The Doctor steps up and lifts your left leg, with his hand beneath the heel, then releases it to fall back on the couch. At least, it is your impression that it falls back.

"'You are not relaxing,' he points out, 'but holding still. When I began to lift your leg, you resisted, and I could feel that it was held stiffly. When I raised and then released it, you did not let it drop, as if it were so much lead. Instead, you actively moved your leg down to the couch. Let's do it over again.'

"Again he raises your leg and again, according to his statement, you fail to let it drop of its own weight. He requests you to practice this at home on future evenings, with the aid of anyone who will help you. . . .

"You need not move or stiffen a part each time before you relax it. Generally the part will be a little tense when you set out to relax. What to do? *Nothing at all.* What do you do with the legs, in order to relax them, after bending down the feet and toes? You let go— relax—go in the negative direction. There it is in a nutshell. You undo in the same manner as in the arms—and that is all. Do not manufacture difficulties. Follow these directions repeatedly," until your next lesson.

PRACTICE PERIOD 4

"Position: On back, with eyelids closed, legs not crossed.

Length of period: Fifty minutes, if you lie without marked restlessness.

Tension: Bend both feet down (at the ankles) and bend down the toes of both feet, all at the same time. Do not bend at the knees.

Relaxation: Let feet and toes go limp suddenly. Continue
                     to rest for several minutes.

Repeat the tension and relaxation and subsequent rest as above
described two more times.
Repeat the tension described above two more times but—
Relax the feet and toes back to their position of test gradually,
requiring one or two minutes for their return.

Caution: While relaxing your legs, try to relax your arms
                     also, farther and farther each minute. But do
                     not move or stiffen your arms before you relax
                     them. Let them go in the negative direction—
                     that is all."

Relaxed Breathing

When you wish to relax the muscles of your breathing apparatus
you can follow these suggestions.

"Position: On your back or, if you prefer, on either side.

Conditions: As previously, a quiet room. Your eyelids are
                     closed and you have been resting quietly for
                     ten minutes.
                     Breath a very little more deeply than usual, but
                     not more than two or three times. Note that
                     your chest is active while you breathe in, but
                     relaxes as you breathe out.

Caution: Do not take a deep breath and do not expel
                     forcibly.

Relaxation: After letting the air come out itself, you are to
                     relax the chest and breathing system. This is
                     readily done, if you will let the chest go, in the
                     same manner as you let the arms and legs go.
                     When you have become relaxed, breathing
                     motions of the chest and abdomen will be slow
                     and slight.

Caution: Make no effort to relax. If at first you don't
                  succeed, try, try again. Breathing will be un-
                  forced, but regular, slow and will go on of
                  itself. But don't force it."

Relaxing the Forehead and Brow

When you are ready to work on the muscles associated with seeing,
you can follow no more helpful suggestions than those of Dr. Jacobson. Lie on your back, preferably on a couch. Get the rest of your
body as relaxed as possible, then wrinkle your brow as you lie there.
After that try to make the muscles of your forehead as loose as those
of your arms and legs. Here are his specific suggestions:

"Preliminary: Stand before a mirror.
              1. Wrinkle forehead, raising eyebrows.
                 Let go gradually, without frowning.
              2. Frown extremely. Let go gradually.
                 See that you do not wrinkle your forehead in
                 attempting to release the frown.

Practice period: Lying with eyes closed.
              1. Wrinkle forehead. Let go extremely, taking
                 several minutes to effect this.
              2. Frown extremely. Let go extremely, taking
                 several minutes to effect this.

Caution: Avoid wrinkling the forehead when trying to
                   efface the frown.

Instruction: While relaxing the forehead and brow, let go
                   the arms, legs and chest extremely, as taught
                   previously.

Caution: . . . do not raise arms or stretch legs or take a
                   deep breath. Relax these parts (without
                   tensing them) while you let go the forehead
                   and brow."

Relaxing the Eyes

"Position: As before, lying on back, eyelids open.

Directions: Look to the right, hold it half a minute, note
                       eyes in action.
                       Letting eyes return to normal position, relax
                       them so, with lids open, for several minutes.
                       Look to the left, then repeat as above.
                       Look up, then repeat as above.
                       Look down, then repeat as above.

Method: Relax your eyes by not bothering to look in
                       any direction. Do not make any effort at all.
                       Avoid holding them.
                       Let your forehead and brow go at the same
                       time, as you learned previously.

Remember: 'Practice makes perfect' and 'Rome was not
                       built in a day.' Be patient as you try to learn.
                       After failures, try again."

Jacobson is interested in removing tension from other areas of the body also. The following techniques are based upon ideas he has given his professional associates. Let us continue the analysis of tensions and make further recommendations for their release in the Jacobson manner:

Relaxing the Organs of Speech

Position: You may lie back in your chair and discover
                       where these tensions are for yourself.

Directions: Say, "Ouch," two or three times. If you pay
                       close attention to sensations in your muscles,
                       you will discover that this single word demands
                       contraction in the upper part of your abdom-

inal wall, in your throat, in your tongue, in the muscles that move your lower jaw, and in your lips. Try saying any other word or phrase. The result will be the same. Then whisper the word. The tensions come back again, though in less degree. Just think the word. They are still to be perceived in the tongue and lips, at least.

Explanation: Logically enough, the muscles of the speech mechanism develop more residual tonus when an individual thinks with words than when he actually speaks. Speech, when it is rhythmic and free flowing, serves as a release device for thoughts. When speech is inhibited, the muscles associated with the formation of words become tense. This tenseness can be released by conscious effort.

Relaxation: Just stop forming words, or even thinking words. Let the lower jaw drop slightly. Keep the tongue quiet. Let the lips become soft. Let the tensions go out of the throat. Breathe rhythmically.

Observation: After a short period of successful practice, thoughts associated with speech will stop forming themselves.

Extraneous tensions which are associated with attention and thinking will be reduced as tensions in the forehead, eyes, mouth, throat, and chest are released. No tensions are more persistent with the use of eyes and with speech than those in the back and neck. Before the whole body can be relaxed, the muscles all along the spine, from the occiput to the sacrum, must lose their hypertonus. This can be achieved only in a reclining position, because these same muscles are used whenever the body is held away from support.

Relaxing the Muscles along the Spine

Position: Lie on the back on a firm support.
            Place the arms at the sides of the body.
            Keep them relaxed.

Tension: Arch the back so that pressure can be felt only
            on the head and on the seat.
            Attend to the sensations of tenseness close to the
            spinal column.
            After holding this extra tenseness for a few
            seconds let about half of it go.
            Then reduce it one half again. Do not jerk the
            body. Release the tension gradually.
            Then reduce the sensation of tautness still
            further until the back is resting again on the
            support.

Relaxation: Continue in the same direction.
            Do not let tenseness recur in any of these
            muscles.
            Make the trunk "lie heavy."

Caution: If necessary for comfort during early practice,
            place a small pillow under the lower back.

Tensions in the muscles of the neck may be very persistent, since a tense person will have postured the head for long periods of time.

Relaxing the Neck

Position: Lie on the back with a slight roll under the
            neck; or rest the neck on the top of an uphol-
            stered chair-back.

Tension: Let the head roll to one side. Then very slowly
            bring it to a mid-line position so that the eyes
            can look directly at the ceiling.

As the head moves, perceive the deep tensions in the neck.

When the head has reached the mid position, let it become unbalanced and roll loosely to the other side.

Repeat once or twice to each side.

Relaxation: Let the head remain quietly in any position it assumes when all tension in the muscles is released.

After learning the techniques suggested for the various regions of the body you must practice them. Some people find it advisable to set aside a definite period each day for this practice. Even a few minutes spent releasing the tension in one region of the body will make a new man of you.

It is far better to find some other time than just before getting into bed at night. If one waits until that time, he may be too tired to practice most effectively, and he may interfere with some of the habits that may be put into effect in conditioning sleep. (See p. 158 f.)

To do nothing is not as easy as it sounds, particularly if the knack has been lost or has never been acquired. Yet it is doing nothing, or relaxing, which permits the body to recoup its losses after a period of effort or even of wakefulness; and it is reducing effort, in the direction of doing nothing, which induces sleep.

6

Psychological Methods of Treatment

EVERYONE'S PROBLEM

SOME OF THE READERS of this book may think that they personally do not need to modify their manner of living to gain relaxation. They think they can continue as they are going, if someone will only give them a trick to be used occasionally. They believe they can keep achieving and producing without giving any concern to recuperation. Although they live in the hectic present and are subject to all its stresses, they believe they can escape its disorganizing influences. Unfortunately, there is no trick to rescue them. They must awaken to the fact that only by learning how to relieve tension at will and by planning activities wisely can anyone achieve a balanced way of life.

No one, when the world about him seems to be going to pieces, can remain serene without working out an orderly scheme under which to live personally. Here are some aids by which to acquire and maintain serenity, as well as vitality, in spite of socio-economic catastrophes. Surely it is not a selfish motive which prompts interest in such efforts, but a sincere desire to uncover the means by which one can "serve best" as well as "live most." Society needs serene as well as dynamic members.

Serenity and dynamic vitality are counterparts, leading man to service for his fellow men as well as happiness for himself. Through serenity one acquires power, not weakness. To be vigorous, when

104

vigor is in order, demands resources of energy which have been acquired through storage during periods of repose and release from previous struggles. The creative, satisfying life calls for periods of relaxation and complete recuperation from effort and strain, alternating with periods of powerful output of mental as well as physical effort. It is only in this sense that one desires to acquire ability to relax—as a preparation for more dynamic outputs of effort. One gains strength through struggle, and one gains strength through repose.

ATTRIBUTES OF A POISED INDIVIDUAL

Four attributes are to be recognized in every individual who has lived dynamically without becoming too tense or hectic—a rhythm in activity exhibiting swings of great output and accomplishment alternating with periods of release from struggle, a sense of values which makes it possible to economize on worthless efforts and minimize strain, an ability to reduce muscular tension in any part of the body consciously whenever desired, and a readiness to fall asleep at will. These four attributes should be the aim of any individual who is tense and in danger of becoming chronically irritable and distraught—a sensible rhythm for activity and repose, a balance of intensities to mark important and unimportant efforts, ability to relax, and ability to sleep when desired.

To describe two antithetical men in middle life will help to make clear advantages of the first two attributes—rhythm between activity and its release, and a sense of values. We will call the first man "Doc." He is healthy, robust, cultured, and refined, of the age when many professional and business men who have been less vigorous than he have broken down. He has reserves of energy at seventy, not because he has guarded his vitality and spent most of his time relaxing, but because he has alternated very vigorous endeavor with intensive rest. He has taxed his strength to its limit, time and time again, in athletic competition in his youth, in grueling work at a desk as a young man, and in long-drawn-out conferences upon which the destiny of many people hinged during his latter years. But, after the physical competition or the mental endeavor or the argument, he has freed his mind of worry and concern, and has immersed himself in true diversion, or has let himself rest completely. For him, diverting social engagements, even at noontime, have broken into the intensity of work; while it has been a frequent occurrence for him, "after work is done," to putter around in his shop polishing some semi-precious stone or hammering out a metal bowl. It has also been his pleasure, evening after evening, to loll back in his favorite chair at home, with pipe in hand and the world's best music coming from record player or radio. He rarely turns on television.

"Doc" has also known what things in his life were important and worth straining for. He has wanted enough money to run a very simple home and to keep a middle-priced car in condition. He has wanted enough with which to educate properly his three energetic children. He has wanted enough to make life comfortable for a lovely wife. He has refused to rush after bonanzas or to confine himself in the gold mine which was his own office. He has wanted a little money to spend, not a lot to hoard; and, as he approaches old age, now that he has "retired" and has been freed from the routine of regular occupation, he can look confidently and enthusiastically into the future, knowing that he can find many thrilling things to interest him and to occupy his time.

Besides knowing how unimportant is work, for itself, he has known how valuable is play. Prudish people have not understood "Doc," for he has had too much fun in living. He has loved laughter, he has loved beauty, he has loved people. He has read so much of current literature as well as the classics that ordinary hardworking professional and business men have often been ashamed when they have found themselves in conversation with him. Furthermore, he has a real acquaintance with modern drama and the world's music. He has been able to acquire all this information because he has considered it worth seeking. He has not worked all his waking time, as have his associates who now are frightened by retirement.

He has not needed to learn special techniques in relaxation. They have been a natural part of his life pattern. He has worked hard. By simple diversions and repose he has "let down" from the accumulated tensions which are associated with all work. When it has come time to go to sleep he has just "closed all the drawers of his mind" and slipped off into limitless unconsciousness. We have described "Doc" because he has so many lessons to teach. Many of us go through life without learning any of them.

Let us take the story of "the big shot in the coal business" as an example of a person who needs to learn these lessons. He met "Doc" once, over a garden fence. "Doc" was working manure into his garden. "Big Shot" was accompanied by a nurse from a retreat for psychologically sick patients. Both men felt sorry for the other one. What "Big Shot" did not know was that "Doc" shoveled manure because he liked to help his flowers. And "Doc" knew how very sick men like "Big Shot" can become.

"Big Shot" had worked "every day of his life," until he was brought to the retreat. To use his own words, he had "been very successful in the coal business," he had "made a lot of money in the coal business." It was the coal business that dominated him. He had not learned to play; he loved nothing but himself and his pot of gold; he knew no music; he had no library; he would get back to the coal business as soon as they would let him "leave this crazy hospital"; he would die in harness. His story is not worth as careful recounting as "Doc's." All he can teach us is in the form of warnings. Yet by studying cases like his we may be stimulated to arrive individually at personal codes to modify our own lives toward living more and serving better.

In times like these it may seem fanciful to stress such qualities as those exhibited by "Doc." Yet the times through which "Doc" has lived have not been very different from the present; except that the present has an intensity and is making an impress of its awfulness on the minds and hearts of men.

IN TIMES OF PEACE AS IN TIMES OF WAR AND REVOLUTION

Men who work in offices in times of peace go through the same motions as men in offices during times of war or revolution. Men who write books in times of peace use the same mechanisms as men who prepare reports and try to chart national courses in times of national stress. Manual laborers and athletes, at any time, must use their bodies and minds in the same manner as mechanics and combatants within a war effort. As well as stamina, these men all need stability; as well as vitality, they all need serenity. In time of war or revolution one needs the same kind of stability and serenity as in peacetime, but in surer amounts, because psychological as well as physical strains are intensified under the stress of killing and preparing to withstand attack. While others are fighting, those individuals who carry on the ordinary work of the world and who give their attention to planning for the future are equally in need of stability and serenity.

If the emphasis in this book is placed upon these latter qualities and not directly upon stamina and vitality, it is because in our society there are too few teachers and preachers emphasizing a truly balanced way of living. Too few leaders of men in industry, business, and the professions, and too few men who are not leaders are sufficiently concerned to seek stability and serenity as a means of offsetting psychophysical breakdowns and actually increasing stamina and vitality. This is a book on how to prevent collapse, not on how to wear out a human machine. This book is on relaxation as an aid in total fitness, not on general hygiene.

There is a phrase, borrowed from the Navy, to emphasize just what qualities are needed particularly in times of emergency. Young men who are taken out of civilian life to serve as naval recruits are told that all the Navy expects of them is conditioning for "more hits, per gun, per minute." What the armed forces want are men who do not run or collapse when they are frightened and who are steady "on the draw." It is a big order, and an order which can not be met alone by stamina and vitality.

It is hard for some of us to accept a slogan coined by the armed forces. There are many sincere and truly fearless people who believe that no problem is ever solved by fighting, and that killing does not get to the roots of a dilemma. Yet, even these individuals may be willing now to think on this theme, "more hits, per gun, per minute," because more accurate and more effective hitting means keener, finer, calmer men at the controls. It is the men, and not the hits, which are our concern. We shall have to trust those men who are at the controls to aim, figuratively, where the shots will be most effective, and so shorten any period of social strain.

MEN VERSUS MATERIAL

Men are more important than material in peacetime as in wartime. If a man's neuromuscular system can be kept working perfectly, even under strain, he will be saved from psychophysical breakdown. While clinging to the theme borrowed from the Navy —more hits, per gun, per minute—we should direct our thinking to the whole area of output for any emergency. All out effort depends upon leaders in community planning and in government, and upon workers and managers in industry. Mere school teachers and workers in offices, as well as the heads of government agencies, and planning commissions, need to keep at their controls under great pressure. Labor and management together must plan how to protect their members from falling down on the job, from becoming inefficient and irritable under strain, from spoiling their work, and from maiming themselves.

In times of social upheaval, as well as in times of war, everyone, not only the industrial worker, comes under stress. Everyone feels the strain. Everyone must do his bit to keep the regime from toppling. In these days, social upheavals seem imminent. It appears that some malcontents want that to happen. The rest of us must rectify the errors in our society, and help one another to bring the ship of state back on keel.

All "workers" in times of stress or national emergency are fighting against two serious odds—the sense of pressure, because what they have to do must be accomplished as speedily as possible; and the sense of fear, because those things they hold dear, even their own lives, may be in danger. Urgency drives a man on but it makes him tense. Fear increases a man's neuromuscular tonus, but it may make him coordinate less well. What can a conditioning program offer to improve an individual's abilities when he is under extreme strain, physical or psychological?

RELAXATION IN A CONDITIONING PROGRAM FOR ADULTS

The more one associates with average men and women in the professions and in business, and the more one tries to advise about techniques in physical fitness for individuals who are driving themselves for maximum output, the more one realizes that the hub of a conditioning program for adults is relaxation. It is not exercise. Next to overeating, as more than one wise physician has said, the body's chief enemy is overexertion.

Thorough students of anatomy and physiology have much cause to be amused at the tremendous concern about large abdomens on the part of both men and women past thirty-five years of age. Presumably, it is a desire to keep fit that prompts this concern. Actually it is a dream of perpetual youth that distresses adults. It is amusing to watch men and women in peacetime cavorting in gymnasiums and disporting themselves in garden togs with the prime motive of slimming their waists. It becomes cause for concern in wartime when Army officers, who are having difficulty keeping down their own rotundities, put the emphasis in a conditioning program on the waistlines of adolescents and young adults. Fortunately, the experiences in gymnasiums and gardens and on parade grounds are often worth-while, even if for other reasons.

Larger waistlines we have as we get older, provided we mature normally and maintain health. What we do not have, as we get older, is ability to coordinate as well as we did in youth. Most of us cannot perform skills demanding balance as well as when we were younger. Our muscles hold their residual tonus a little longer unless we have learned to release that hypertonus. There need be no lessening in courage with increasing age nor a reduction in ability for mental learning, but the ability to master complicated new psychomotor skills and to maintain those already learned appears to wane.

There are many people in the middle or late adult age group, however, who must be kept in optimum psychomotor condition because much is expected of them physically as well as mentally. How may we help them to maintain their coordinating abilities at greatest efficiency? The answer is by helping them to get rid of hypertonus in muscular tissues before incoordination and infinitesimal quivering set in.

SUGGESTIONS FROM ATHLETIC TRAINERS

We may turn to athletic trainers for advice. They, more than other specialists, know how to keep bodies up to coordinated and maximum output under gruelling circumstances. They have to know how to teach their charges how to relax. It is well known that ability to relax in certain regions of the body during any athletic performance is beneficial for perfect performance, and that skill in relaxing totally before and after a match is important for the one who must conserve energy and recuperate readily after effort. Yet trainers have to be constantly helping athletic performers in relaxing. When they are competing or when they even think of competing, they tend to get tense. Successful athletes may be able to maintain composure and to relax at will, but "runners up," of whom there are hundreds to one winner, are always excited and on edge. As hard as athletic trainers have tried to teach their trainees to relax, they have been unable to offset the tensing effects of competition. This almost unavoidable tenseness is the main reason why the best athletes have massage for their limbs, before and after strenuous effort; why they take warm or mildly cool showers after events; and why they try to divert their minds from the matter at hand just before the contest, at least. They must have mastered psychological as well as physical techniques for optimum condition and output.

Industrial and mental workers might also try mild heat and soothing massage after work, along with properly selected exercises (see Chapter 5), to keep the circulation adequate and to prevent the congestion which may be visualized as the cause of much discomfort and inefficiency in muscles and joints. This combination of physical agents has had a very good reputation ever since the age of Hippocrates. Today, as in the highday of Greek culture, the wisest of the hard-working business men and politicians, as well as athletes, have known what it means to go to a gymnasium or a spa to be kept in psychophysical condition and free from bodily discomforts. The wonder is that less wise individuals have still be be urged to try these simple, although time-consuming, techniques for total fitness unless they are concerned about their weight and the size of their waistlines.

Possibly the main reason why busy people, through the ages, have had to be encouraged and instructed to get such simple and natural measures as heat, massage, and exercise and mental diversion for the relief of less severe yet chronic discomforts is that these techniques are so time consuming. But therein lies one of their great advantages over drugs and substitutes for nature's own methods. The people who have the chronic complaints for which these devices would afford adequate relief are the very ones who need to have a respite from tensing occupations. They are not the country folk and ordinary manual laborers who have physical work to do each day, and are satisfied with a simple routine. The chronic complainers from frayed nerves, taut muscles, and inflexible joints in normal times as well as in times of stress, are the high-powered magnates of industry, the conscientious statesmen, the overzealous toilers in the professions, the dissatisfied social climbers, who sit glued to their chairs for hours and who think that every moment of their waking time should be spent in remunerative or "worth-while" work. They do not acknowledge that periods of recreation, or diversion, or nonremunerative occupation are worth while also.

How can we educate people to realize that they must have physical and mental diversion in order to be balanced? How can we impress upon them the ultimate futility of a life given only to work and anxiety? There lies the crux of the matter. As everyone who tries to help tense people knows, grown men and women should recapture the spirit of childhood occasionally, to offset their periods of serious effort. As was indicated in Chapter 4, psychically tense individuals represent a type which is the antithesis of the child. They have single-track minds. They cannot play. It is play they need in their leisure time as well as creative hobbies and purposeful activites, to enrich an otherwise drab existence. The shorter the periods for leisure, at a time of national or personal crisis, the more those periods should be spent in almost frivolous escape.

RELEASE THROUGH PLAY

Real refreshment may be had through play, because in true play one cannot take self too seriously. "Play," as here used, does not mean participating in an activity to win. It does not connote competition. Athletic trainers, on the other hand, do not think that their contests are play. They know that they are not. To participate in any game or sport, with a grim determination to win, is not to play; and the trainers, coaches, and contestants know it. Still adults often consider such activity to be the only justifiable form of "play" after childhood.

It is unfortunate that so many men are under the impression that they were playing when they were fighting on high school or college teams. It was called playing. This is the reason why some ex-athletes go to their clubs to work for cups in handball or tennis. Others go just because they are still adolescent and want to show off. If either group works hard enough to win over strong opponents, they are not playing. They are still struggling. They may be gaining benefits, to be sure, but they are not playing. If it is play they need, to offset work, they must get it under conditions of less dourness.

In leisure time adults need to take the edge off their strivings, not add more strivings. When they go to gymnasiums, the mature ones go to have fun. Sometimes they play one kind of game; sometimes they play another. They want to feel better when they get home. They want to be refreshed, not worn out. They want to have all grouchiness dispelled. They do not want to chalk up scores for the day. They do not care much whether they win or lose. All the average adult really should be looking for is fun and a mild workout. If one is seeking diversion he must beware of the person who hangs around the gymnasium or court just to beat another at the one game in which he can excel. It is not worth while to struggle against such an opponent unless all one wants is sweat and exhaustion.

REST PAUSES

Rest pauses, as well as wisely spaced periods of exercise and diversion, will help prevent excess tension, and psychophysical stress and

inefficiency. When are we going to learn that the human body, like
any animal body, is a dynamic, moving body, but that it cannot
tolerate continuous effort of any kind long without rest pauses?
Edward L. Thorndike was not far from the fundamental truths that
we are seeking when he was studying mental fatigue years ago.*
What we are concerned about is just what he was concerned about;
but we are calling it psychophysical fatigue which affects our "hitting" score, not our thinking score. Thorndike tells us that, to protect the mind, the body needs rest pauses and sleep, frequent changes
of position and movement, and social intercourse. Professional
people in their trades, manual laborers in construction trades,
fighters in killing trades, and all others like them, must be given
opportunities to offset the tensions inherent in their work by rest
pauses, as well as by changes in occupation and by sociability.

Just how the rest pauses should be spaced, for every trade and
occupation, is not known; nor whether cots should be provided, nor
whether legs should be raised above the hips, nor whether eyes
should be closed. It is known, however, that there must be rest
pauses of psychological as well as physical import. Physicians and
teachers must put honest study upon such problems as rhythm
for work, length and spacing of mealtimes, provisions for psychological "letdown," etc., etc. Their findings must be given wider
distribution than such studies have ever had before.

DIVERSION AND LETDOWN

Through the realization of Thorndike's plea for social intercourse
will come psychological "letdown." There should be a particular
respect for laughter. Not only will laughter do more for the diaphragm and the whole circulation than any other form of physical
activity, but it also will psychologically offset fear and concern. No
people need more to learn how to laugh than the Anglo-Nordics.
They rarely laugh in simple abandon. Laughter and the long view
that comes with it might get closer to a mechanism for controlling

---

* Thorndike, Edward L. *Educational Psychology*, Vol. III: *Mental Work and
Fatigue.* New York: Teachers College, Columbia University, 1926.

our moods and our drives, our attitudes toward ourselves and toward our destinies than anything else with which we could experiment.

LAUGHTER

To laugh is to relieve the constant heavy downward pull of the sense of inferiority. Among healthy children, laughter can be accounted for by feelings of extreme well-being, as well as by high spirits. In adults it is an expression of successful, faultless adaptation to the environment, as well as of health. For an example, when a person laughs at someone else slip on a banana peel and fall, it is because he himself did not do so, because he did not lose control of himself.

It is true that we laugh a lot more when we are in robust health than when we are ailing. Is is possible that physical and psychological aspects of health are closely interrelated through laughter, and that laughter can be a cause of physical health as well as an expression of psychological well-being? Does laughter not relax the entire body, as well as the mind? As any physician can testify, it is more effective than a drug, when a tonic is needed. So laughter can be used as an aid to health, when aids are necessary, and as an expression of health, when expression is in order.

We do not laugh only to be well, or to tell the world that we are healthy. We laugh also when we feel that we are masters of a situation or safe from a predicament which might have engulfed us, like the banana peel. Unfortunately, very few people feel superior in their work, so very few people laugh or sing at their work. They have to find laughter in their leisure time.

Humor is of immense value as a recreative experience, and sometimes as a refuge for those overcome by panic and fear. Mirth-provoking jokes shake us loose from our cares, while quips and wholesome pranks make us light-hearted and gay. If we need humor, we may also need to go out of our way to find it. It does not lurk around every corner. But it is to be found in moving picture houses and in theaters not too far distant, or in books which have been written for the very purpose of giving vent to the author's zest for living, and with the intention of bringing its readers up from the doldrums. Do not be ashamed to go off the beaten track to find laughter.

Possibly we should take a lesson from the Chinese. Word came from the Eastern Front during World War II that the Chinese organized dramatic squads to entertain and divert men when they came away from combat. Surely pantomime and other forms of play acting, interspersed through all our fretful days, would bring as high returns to those in positions of management and to those in positions of labor as to those in the armed services.

THE NEED FOR HOBBIES

Public theater and amateur dramatics fall within the province of hobbies. These are two forms of diversion which have always appealed to people of property and to intellectuals. This is what makes them worth emphasizing in a book of this kind, because tension is very common in those groups. Individuals who have not had advanced schooling, or who do not have to apply themselves to mental problems, or who have not inherited or acquired positions in the financial and professional worlds are inclined to believe that those who have done so do not have to work very hard, are play-boys and follow the entertainment circuit because they have the money and are trying to show off. This is not the case. People in these classes carry a great deal of the real burden of society and their class has learned that the entertainment offers them escape and refreshment. An aside at this point is that leaders in the labor movement and even hot-heads for social change are seen, more and more, to be in the highly intelligent class; and to come, more and more, into the same company with those who desire and can pay for public entertainment.

At home they, even more than sophisticates, have television to while away their hours of leisure. Television is a tremendous industry which would not have developed if there had not been a need for escape from reality and surcease from care and boredom. TV, in its role as a news medium, may be a public address system for politicians and news sources, but it has come to its level of efficiency and artistic perfection only because of its role as an entertainment medium.

TV is effective as an escape device because it enlists both the visual and the auditory senses in the comprehension of it. It calls for the same sensory involvement as theatre, plus a more favorable if unconscious tactual state of being. How often has the theatre or opera spectator thought, "Oh, how I wish I could be in a more comfortable chair, have on more comfortable clothes, have my feet raised and a pillow under my head." All these he can have when he watches television at home.

That radio and record playing are becoming popular again is a very good sign, as far as need for relaxation is concerned. They can be comprehended solely by auditory attention; they do not demand visual concentration or static positioning. Those who have no need to throw their whole sensorium into the act of escape from reality will gain comfort and release from them.

As the twentieth century draws to a close, it will be worth watching what forms of entertainment come to the fore. Will they provide louder, more discordant stimuli to crowd out reality, and whip the recipients into more hectic states; or quieting, more soothing experiences to reveal that the world can be in less turmoil and be less stressful for its citizens?

Dramatics and music will surely be continued as sources of expression and of refreshment in the society of the future. What about other hobbies?* Hobbies are properly defined as any engrossing topic, object or plan to which one constantly reverts; or any occupation or interest to which one gives his spare time, not his earning time. Once committed to a hobby, the average individual pursues it, or some interest it leads into, until the end of his days. One may make things as a hobby, but one may also just study about something as a hobby.

As far as the manipulative hobbies, like crafts and painting and furniture refinishing, are concerned, little need be said except to stress that they are of value for individuals who are not in a rehabilitation setting as well as for those who have nothing else to do with

* Rathbone, Josephine L. and Lucas, Carol. *Recreation in Total Rehabilitation.* Springfield: Charles C Thomas, 1959 (Chap. 12, Hobbies).

long hours in hospital or school for the handicapped or old folks' home.

A warning is in order if hobbies are to be effective for ordinary, tense individuals. These must not be used just to put off tasks which one has no desire to attack. When a college professor has a bunch of papers to correct, he must not go out for a game of golf. When a homemaker has letters to be written or the ironing to be done, she must not go to a friend's, on the spur of the moment, to play bridge. When an author has set himself the stint of 1000 or 5000 words per day, he cannot excuse himself by getting his stamp collection into better shape.

If hobbies are to be used 'to ease stress, they must be used consciously as rewards for work accomplished or for tasks finished. This will take planning and self management. Herein resides the whole secret of relaxation by psychological devices, as will be shown before the end of this chapter. Some relief for tension may be gained through the efforts of someone else, who tells a funny story or is responsible for a diversion; but any really meaningful and easily to be repeated psychological device for relaxing will have to be self controlled. Someone else may have to set the tense individual on the track of a relaxing hobby and keep him practicing it until he takes it over as one of his own methods of getting rid of tension. But in the long run he will have to use his hobby when he knows he should, after he has become tense and not to escape doing a task that is his. The recreation leader, who desires to help a patient acquire a hobby, must understand the temperament of the patient and know the location where the patient must function, the equipment and amount of space he may have at his disposal, and the amount of money he can be encouraged or allowed to spend.

The recreation leader is going to have very little difficulty in getting the average patient to make something with his hands if he can see what other people are able to fashion, but it may be harder to help him collect things or to study some phase of nature. But he is going to test his powers of observation toward their limits in finding hobbies adjusted to the aptitudes and temperaments and resources of all his patients.

Some people react primarily to things they can look at, and like to have beautiful things around them. As collectors, they go in for the accumulation of items that attract the eye, such as porcelains, buttons and prints. Others prefer objects with historical significance, and therefore would collect things that come from the past and show an evolutionary trend, such things as antique furniture, old specimens of printing or theater bills and even bizarre, primitive sculpture. For the mechanically inclined there are gadgets and handmade objects like toy airplanes and ship models to be made. Those who favor nature may choose something like minerals or insects. For ear appeal, there is music and rare phonograph records. There are even collectors items with nose appeal; some devotees hoard unusual perfumes from all over the world.

The recreation specialist, trying to interest a person in a new collecting hobby should consider whether or not it is going to be possible for him to pursue it on his own or after he leaves the special school or rehabilitation center. Should he be encouraged to collect bulky things like old bicycles? If he does, where will he keep them? Can he rent a barn with access to a secluded country road, where the more daring of his friends will try to ride the contraptions? Instead, should he be encouraged to become interested in clippings from the daily newspaper—pictures or advertisements, possibly of automobiles or other vehicles.

There is much to be said in warning about the expense of some collections. Should a patient even be encouraged to become interested in the covers of expensive magazines if he is attracted toward oil painting, for example? Can he afford to become interested in coins? That quest leads toward doubloons or other gold pieces which are both rare and very expensive, and which should be under guard in museums.

This point can become very important. Everyone should have a good idea about what he can afford to spend on a collection. It is well to point out to the beginning collector that there are many items worth collecting that require very little money. Naturally, the beautiful collections that finally get placed in museums cost thousands of dollars; but, for every millionaire specialist, there is a vast army of ordinary collectors, whose sole pleasure is in collecting the things that they can easily afford.

When a person can become crazy about something, it is usually hard to keep him from collecting samples. Even if they are perishable or repulsive to other people he will want them. Witness the way a little child collects brightly colored autumn leaves and does nothing to protect them from withering and blowing away, or frogs and mice which he cannot protect from the housekeeping proclivities of his mother. Collecting is for having: that is all.

What people love is often inexplicable, but that they should love something is imperative for good health. Some people collect scraps of ribbon and lace only because they are pretty. There are others who would fill all possible spaces in the house with tropical fish, not because of an interest in this form of life, but only because of the gorgeous coloring these fish display and their rapid movements. Others have bird boxes of all possible sizes and shapes because they actually love birds: they are so gay and entertaining.

The collecting items mentioned so far—leaves, slimey and furry creatures, furbelows and shelters for miniature forms of life against the elements—are only suggestions to help us tie collecting to the beauty inherent in nature. The casual observer, watching a collector as he pores over his "treasures," is often moved to inquire, "What can he see in such things?" The answer, of course, is that just as love among human beings is far from being a simple emotion, so the love of the collector for his collection is a complex and wondrous attachment. It is important to realize that to most collectors the collection, on its way to completion, takes on a life and character of its own. To its creator it truly becomes a living thing, and its component parts also become the objects of the collector's real attachment. For some items for collections national organizations are in existence, and for all of them local clubs can be organized easily, where fellow-collectors can get together and compare notes or trade items. Thus a framework can be established into which a simple device like a collecting hobby can be set.

If we would only throw some of our energies into such channels we would find ourselves refreshed to return to our imposed tasks. We would also find it more easy to relax at will, for our tensions would have been modified and changed rather than intensified.

GROUP COUNSELLING

Now we come to the heart of this chapter: a method by which psychological aids for relaxing can be passed on and become effective for any individual who is experiencing stress. Every person who needs to modify his way of life and to get a new point-of-view must do so on his own power. He must make the changes himself. To take drugs will never help him get to the root of his trouble; all the best of them can do is to calm him down, and they may not help him think clearly. To rely upon someone else's ideas will never be more than superficial; one has to agree with counsel and put new ideas into practice to have them affect conduct. But how can a teacher or physician bring about changes in another's thinking and behaving?

During the past two decades a great deal of credit has been given to "group therapy" in changing ways of thinking and behaving. Psychiatrists, psychologists, other workers in the mental-health professions, social workers, and educators, clergymen, and guidance counsellors in schools and industrial plants have been exploring the possibility of reaching people in groups, to change their ways of thinking and to bring them mental help. Patients have been reached in psychiatric institutions and in mental health clinics; social diverts have been reached in prison and in homes for delinquent youths; people who have sought help have been reached in nudist camps and in more conventional centers organized or modified just for this purpose. The approach has been made through psychodrama, through group recreational activities like dancing and singing, through just sitting in circles and holding hands, by looking into each other's eyes and touching each other, by swimming in the nude, by crying together, and by talking, talking, talking. The last method has been the one most generally used.

When patients are already in an institution, it is not difficult to get them into groups. They can just be conducted to the meeting place. To attract their interest may not be easy, but most people would rather be in the company of others than isolated. The solitary person can just be placed near. Then the skill of the leader is tested to make him communicate and cooperate. When people are not in an institution and when they are seeking help for a personal problem, it is often hard to induce them to enter a group. They will do so more readily if the organization behind the group has a fashionable name. The Syanon and Esalen centers have this advantage. Also, the fact that counselling can be less expensive in groups than individually may be an inducement.

Each group has a leader, who knows the expressed or suspected needs of each member, and whose business it is to carry the thought of the group, to reflect the suggestions of the members, to keep track of the contributions of each, and to keep notes for future reference. Each leader works out a method which suits best his training and orientation. He finds the way that works best for him. Many leaders have been influenced by Freudian hypotheses and methodology. Some are members of the American Group Psychotherapy Association.

Some leaders, who like unstructured sessions, think they get the best results if the groups are fairly homogeneous—borderline psychopaths who are using tranquilizers in the daytime and sleeping pills at night, a group with family centered problems, married couples who have contemplated divorce, folks past fifty-five years of age who are threatened by retirement, discontented housewives, discouraged businessmen, etc., etc. Other leaders are able to reach groups of people whose initial problems are various. They may or may not structure their sessions more carefully.

In almost all groups the membership is shifting, because a leader usually has a private practice, also, from which he feeds in patients. Furthermore, he wants to help a patient leave therapy as soon as he is able. It is well to put a limit on the duration of a series of sessions; and the period for each session is limited, say an hour, and the number of these periods is predetermined and regular.

From the patient's point-of-view the group is often less threatening than a therapist alone. The patient is less aware of the decisions he is making than of the changes he observes others to be making. He is comforted by the fact that other members in the group have problems somewhat like his. He often enjoys sharing his troubles, the superficial ones at least.   He does not realize how much these superficial troubles tell the trained leader.   A person so often reveals his deeper needs when someone else in the group is unburdening his problems.   Too often a person does not or cannot ask for the help he really needs, directly, because he does not understand his basic need or has hidden or submerged it.

Group psychotherapy can be less expensive than individual psychotherapy, to be sure, but it is also more subtle.   It reveals problems indirectly and offers treatment or insight indirectly.   All therapists who use groups admit this fact.   Therapists who find it difficult to be indirect in their approach had best use the group method.   Also, a therapist can take a great deal more transference in a group than in private sessions.   The group protects him from hurtful transference, manual or verbal; and he is able to slip away without enduring affectionate or pugnacious transference, leaving the patient to admit his transference to others who can temper it.

In a group the leader can be more of a spectator.   He can sit apparently as a visitor, and only reflect ideas and opinions offered by others.   He can assure that "everything is going to work out all right."   He can sit passively, saying nothing in a group when it would be awkward to do so in a private session.   He can change the focus of attention by rising to open or close a window or offer cigarettes.   He can laugh to make light of a suggestion, or offer praise when encouragement is needed or insight has been gained.   He may be more effective in a group situation than privately.   He can help more people to reach decisions for themselves when he works through groups.   For helping tense people restructure their lives, group therapy is the method to be preferred.

While the exercise and conscious relaxing program is being developed through regular sessions in groups, psychological techniques can be interspersed with the physical techniques; or the subjects can meet only in separate sessions with the leader for thinking through the problems which make people tense.

I have conducted such sessions for many years.   I am so satisfied with the group method for psychological guidance that I will never try again to help a tense person individually.   Anyone who wishes to lead a group in counselling for relaxing purposes should study carefully Chapters 2 to 5 and select, for his group, the topics to start discussion in a series of sessions.

No one can get rid of his tensions unless he faces the causes of his distress, and modifies his way of life to rectify them. I have found that the safest and easiest way to help a person to face reality, and to establish a new set of values and a new pattern of conduct, is through *group* discussion of the problems that are quite universal in my own trainees. I have been trained to recognize true psychotics; and these I refer to a psychiatrist. In a group it is easier for the leader not to give direct advice, but to make it possible for members of the group to figure out for themselves what may be their faults in thinking and in behaving. And, by sharing faults voluntarily with others, the members of the group are assisted in improving their own behavior.

OBSERVATION OF NERVOUS MANNERISMS

A good way to start a discussion of possible causes of tension in any of us is to describe for each other the usual signs of neuromuscular tension—fidgeting, tapping fingers, pacing the floor, frowning, fixed stare, clenching fists and jaws, holding head on one side, curling feet and legs around chair legs, shrill speech or hesitancy in speech, irritability, etc.

The leader of the group may choose to treat the group as a seminar and have the members bring to class, as it were, a list of ideas for each discussion. The information each one offers may describe himself or some other individual whom he sees frequently and whom he would like to help. It is often easier for a trainee to show concern at first, for someone else; but before the seminar is completed, each person in it will be directly or indirectly studying himself. The prepared reports on assigned topics can be handed to the group leader at the beginning of a session, kept in confidence by him, but drawn upon for discussion in the group or in private conference later.

During the session when nervous mannerisms are being discussed, the leader will show that movements really are relief devices, and that the truly tensing mannerisms are the held positions.

Then each member of the group, before the next meeting, can study himself, or his selected subject, to find out what his residual tensions are.

DISCUSSION OF PHYSICAL COMPLAINTS

After describing the one he is studying, as far as his tensions are concerned, the group member should list his physical complaints. He may see immediately a relationship between his held positions and his aches and pains. Or he may associate his discomforts with old injuries or operations of which he is still being protective, or with posturing at his desk or on his job.

ONE'S DAILY HABITS

In connection with one's daily occupation, the most important factor as far as tension is concerned is his schedule. Everyone has twenty-four hours in every day, and those who arrange that time wisely are free from distress and tension.

As to eating, in our culture it is usually more important *when* we eat than *what* we eat. Of course it is important that we drink enough milk, for the calcium in milk is important for the proper functioning of nerves and muscles. Probably stimulating drinks, like coffee and Coca-Cola, should be kept to a moderate amount.

As to relaxants, like wine and beer, the group leader must be careful not to moralize. In a series of group discussions, everything and anything can be aired, but nothing should be condemned unless the entire group makes that decision. As far as liquor is concerned, the dependency of some people on the cocktail hour, to offset the tensions of the day, may be offered in discussion. The leader may inject some indication of regret that these people are so unresourceful as not to be able to find other more creative and less destructive devices for let-down, devices which allow them to remain in control of themselves.

Two other devices which are to be preferred for relief from the day's tension are general exercise and sleep. Why don't tense people use these properly?

At this point in the group counselling, the discussion hits a high note. The group may be taken unaware when it learns so simply that tense people often have to re-evaluate what is good for them. They must not be compulsive about their rules for personal hygiene, of course. These rules may even be quite flexible. Yet, all of us must have rules which give us great satisfaction and true pleasure when they are obeyed.

ONE'S LIKES AND DISLIKES

A session on the likes and dislikes of the members of a group is always very amusing as well as very enlightening—amusing because what other people dislike is always funny, and enlightening because it becomes obvious that one's own dislikes must seem funny to someone else. Just contemplate aversions like eating berries out of a glass sauce dish, or sitting in a room with green wallpaper, or picking up a burnt match stick. These aversions may be so great that they cause nausea or make one turn one's back on them. When they are revealed as personal idiosyncracies, however, they often vanish.

What about likes and dislikes of one's own body? For example, a girl's dislike of her plump underdeveloped body configuration, a small man's desire to be large and strong, as an indication of manhood. These concepts may be very disturbing indeed until it is learned that one's feelings about them are not unique, because they are culturally oriented. Each person may be able to face his own feelings about his own body better after a group session when such disturbing dislikes are brought into the open for discussion, and are shown to be quite normal and quite general.

Take the aversion to burnt match sticks, for example. Once upon a time, when one woman with that strong dislike was a little girl, her parents and beloved baby brother were far from home, for her father's vacation, and she came down with pleurisy. She was very, very sick; the minister came to pray with her grandmother, who was taking care of her; then the doctor wired her parents to come home; the next thing she knew her father was sitting next to her bed with his big, cool hand on her forehead, telling her a story; her baby brother had been discovered near a fireplace, with an empty match box in his lap and burnt match sticks all around him; he might have destroyed the cottage where the folks were spending their vacation and killed himself. The vivid recall of that series of events, and another during a Children's Day Program, a few months later, when she completely forgot the poem she was to recite at the moment she glanced down from the front of the stage to see burnt match sticks all over the matting covered floor in front of the kerosene footlights, and her father coming down an aisle to "save" her, cleared up forever her odd but sickening and tensing aversion. Episodes like these, tied in with dependence on and gratitude toward a revered individual, as well as excessively strong emotional attachment to a loved one, when recalled in their entirety, help one to lose compulsive fears and difficult-to-explain dislikes.

After discussing a few strong dislikes, which have been sources of great embarrassment and tension to individuals, it becomes apparent to every group member that few great socioeconomic or even international problems, which threaten the stability of the world, have as much influence for each individual as his own petty idiosyncracies. The self is revealed as petty and superficial. How much better it would be to get control of oneself, to be calm and composed, to have a sense of humor, and therefore to have less useless tension.

PLACE OF LOVE AND RELIGION IN LIFE

At the end of any series of sessions in group counselling for tense people, it is not strange that the group members usually come around to discussing their basic attitudes to life, to their fellow men, to love and to ultimate religious and philosophical questions. Emotional and spiritual factors in a conditioning program are no less important than the psychophysical ones mentioned above. As we think of satisfying and quieting experiences in personal lives, we think first of love. For the adult man or woman who is caught in the vortex of a cyclonic effort to rebuild a society and a world, no source of personal help is greater than love.

Just as tense people reveal disturbances in their relationships with others, so well-adjusted individuals reveal satisfaction in the fulfillment of their needs for love and friendliness. Whereas lack of affection may be a cause of tension, satisfying affectional relationships may be a remedy or "cure." The import of love must not be lost sight of in a chapter on psychological aids to poise and composure.

One timely suggestion may be added, growing out of woman's experience. She has a lesson to teach the world about love. As man has given woman an opportunity to share in his education and in his work, he must let her share with him her greater wisdom about love. The greatest difficulty in love affairs is the original selection of the recipient for love. Women are no cleverer than men in choosing the objects of their love. Possibly women have not had enough experience in this realm, since through the ages they have taken a more passive role than men. They have waited to be selected. If their passivity has given them fewer opportunities to choose mates, it has also made them more anxious to keep their mates when they have found them. Men have always broken the bonds of love affairs and of marriages more readily than women. They have grown tired of old loves. Also they have been more selfish in loving, and therefore have gained less than they might have from love.

Man has been too hasty and too eager for a climax in love. He has not valued the less exciting concomitants of love and has not learned to appreciate love in a diffuse form. The masculine or the strong way of love is intense and quickly passed. The feminine or more receptive way of love is less intense but longer lasting. Man's way of love is like a fast-moving river. Woman's way of love is like the river bank. The world, and man within it, need the stability of woman's kind of love.

The more passive qualities of devotion and self-sacrifice are woman's, not man's. Her deep placidity, which is needed for the nourishing and storing of life, is also needed for the healing of man's wounds, inflicted by his own cruelty and thoughtlessness. Woman's power must move out from the confines of her own home into the greater world home if that realm is ever to become stable. Just as women are called upon to make havens or homes to which their individual men can come periodically for refreshment and surcease from care, so must woman's way provide the world with an escape from power politics and eventual disorganization. Woman's world is the human world. Woman's world is the world of love.

Rabindranath Tagore carried still further this suggestion for the need of woman's way in the world of affairs. Instead of the masculine or economic way of power politics and efficiency, he said that we need the feminine or spiritual way of reciprocity and love. In religious life, we have had an example of living and service through love. Cannot this Christlike principle be carried into world-wide social cooperation? (See pp. 153 and 154.) In the West as well as in the India of Tagore there are champions of the way of love. Their voices have been indistinct in the past, only because the din of other, raucous, voices has drowned them. Now these voices, like the vibrant one of Martin Luther King, must be listened to, or the magnificent and sacrificial output in material and human resources of past wars and of the United Nations will have been in vain.

One of the many admonitions of Christ which we must learn to follow is, "Love thy neighbor as thyself." Loving people unlike ourselves will purge our own souls of selfcenteredness and smugness, and free our minds to learn of them. They have much to teach us—our distant Chinese and Indian neighbors, as well as the dark-skinned people in our midst. We might turn to them for suggestions to offset our greatest cause of tension—our willingness to wear out our neuromuscular systems in overwork and hectic play.

American Indians and Negroes, to take just two groups, have much to teach us. We have never looked beneath the surface into the core of their beings, as they may not have looked beneath ours. In the past, they have accepted our aggressiveness and our sense of superiority, however, with much more charity than we would show toward others who consider themselves to be our superiors. In the present it would be worth while for us to analyze the resources they have had in adversity and the composure we have expected of them when there has been provocation to violence. May it have lain, in the past, in their lack of striving for great material rewards? May it have been fostered by their ready response to rhythm through their songs and dances? They had something to teach us, the American Negroes, in their readiness to laugh and their escape into

the inner man. We and they may have lost too much as they have
become like us.

ISOLATION AND MEDITATION

Let us seek to become less sophisticated. Less highly "civilized"
men have one characteristic in common with great philosophers.
They desire to spend time by themselves. They like to look at life
occasionally rather than stay ever in its midst. They know how to
meditate. Thinking for them is not always a struggle, for they allow
plenty of time for ideas to work themselves out. Would that more
sophisticated individuals would learn of simple people and of philosophers to put some period aside each day for meditation and calm
reasoning. Our Puritan forefathers did so at morning prayers.
Certain new religious cults have emphasized the value of the quiet
hour when they look for guidance. But the majority of modern folk
take no time for meditation, or for prayer.

How badly we need isolation and meditation occasionally. They
provide psychological relaxation and refreshment. The effect is
quieting. There are two essential conditions for the progress of an
individual—relative isolation and discipline. No one has practiced
these conditions as well as the searcher after truth on the shores of
Galilee. No one has understood better than He the power to be
derived from isolation. "When he had sent the multitude away, he
went up into the mountain apart . . . and when the evening was
come, he was there alone" (Matthew 14:23). Would that he could
teach us to respect his way! No one has ever been more disciplined
than He. No one ever understood better the balanced way of life,
with friendships and appreciations to offset hardships and trials.
Would that all troubled people would go to His footstool to learn of
Him. He can show the way, the truth, the light.

We strivers and doers may have to face the unwelcome fact that
not even we can always be achieving successfully. We may have to
adjust to the fact that, in order to do our best at the top of our curve
of energy, we must consent to be at far less than our best for long
stretches of time. Provided we keep free from organic illness, provided we give ourselves enough rest and diversion, and provided

we seek spiritual sources of power and tranquillity, our energies will soar again after periods of escape from striving; and we shall be once more the most dynamic sons of men.

> Dear Lord and Father of Mankind
>   Forgive our feverish ways.
> Reclothe us in our rightful mind;
> In purer lives Thy service find,
>   In deeper reverence praise.
>
> In simple trust like theirs who heard,
>   Beside the Syrian sea,
> The gracious calling of the Lord,
> Let us, like them, without a word,
>   Rise up and follow thee.
>
> O Sabbath rest by Galilee!
>   O calm of hills above!
> Where Jesus knelt to share with Thee
> The silence of eternity,
>   Interpreted by love.
>
> Drop Thy still dews of quietness,
>   Till all our strivings cease;
> Take from our souls the strain and stress,
> And let our ordered lives confess
>   The beauty of Thy peace.
>
> Breathe through the heats of our desire
>   Thy coolness and Thy balm;
> Let sense be dumb, let flesh retire;
> Speak through the earthquake, wind, and fire,
>   O still small voice of calm!

Whittier—1872

7

Relaxation and Sleep for Therapy

IF WE ARE TO DISCUSS sleep and relaxation in the same book, we must explain in how far they are alike and in how far they are different. The low level of motor activity is the most striking sign of sleep; but sleep does not always bring relaxation, and even deep relaxation can be achieved without sleep. When one learns how to relax, however, one does sleep better; and most people have reason to recognize a close relationship between satisfactory relaxation and ability to sleep.

"SLEEP THERAPY"

So much emphasis has been placed on sleep therapy since 1960, however, that it would be inappropriate to present a book on relaxation at this time without discussing sleep. It must be stated at the outset that there have been many misconceptions that patients have to lose consciousness and actually "fall asleep" to gain benefits from what has been called "sleep therapy." Actually, more typically they achieve deep relaxation and drowsiness.

The one thing that sleep gives is cerebral inhibition. Here we go back to the teaching of Pavlov. He was convinced that sleep, hypnosis and hysteria represented different types and degrees of inhibition, which allow for physiological repair of cortical cells and protect them from the danger of being destroyed as a result of excessive demands. Pavlov was first and foremost a physiologist. He saw psychosis and neurosis as a fault in brain tissue, with hysteria as a protection against more damage, and hypnosis and sleep as means of treating the same. He favored sleep.

Pavlov gave credit to the early treatment suggestions of S. Weir Mitchell,[1] who put his neurasthenic patients to bed for long periods, with overfeeding to build up their "fat and blood," and daily massage to take the place of exercise. Since Pavlov's day there has been an Institute of Therapy in the Academy of Medical Sciences, in Moscow, to continue his teachings and the research he started. The Russians have done more than anyone else to explore the various ways of inducing sleep for medical purposes.

Whereas a Pavlovian claims that physical sleep prevents the brain from being damaged or helps it to recover from trauma, and a Freudian says that in sleep we enter a condition as similar as possible to intrauterine life, the ordinary individual sees nothing more unusual in sleep than the shutting off of consciousness. Just that is precious to him. He believes that the preservation of a regularly recurring sleep cycle is imperative for the maintenance of his health.

MECHANISMS OF SLEEP

During sleep one's mind and body become refreshed. Possibly it is the tired body that takes the reluctant brain along for a forced rest, or possibly it is the cumulated consequences of organized thinking which demand that the body stop moving and rest. At least they rest together, the mind and body, during sleep.

Ever since it was possible to study the cellular structure (anatomy) and function (physiology) of the brain, scientists have been trying to decide where in the brain is the "seat" of sleep. It is now thought that sleep and wakefulness are controlled in the reticular formation, or tiny nerve network in the brain stem. Trunks of all the great sensory nerves converge in the reticular formation, so that sensory signals feed through the reticular formation. It serves as "a vigilant sentinel, a general alarm system, a pacemaker for the rest of the brain . . . keeping the cortex awake"[2] or letting it sleep. (See p. 40.)

Sleep has been studied by deprivation experiments, which have shown the consequences of going without sleep; but also by electro-encephalograms (EEG), which have revealed the brain activity during sleep. During 80 per cent of sleeping time the electro-encephalographic pattern is of large amplitude, slow waves with spindle spurts. This is known as "light" sleep, and it is thought to represent inhibition of activity of the cerebral cortex. During the other 20 per cent of sleeping time the EEG pattern is of low amplitude, fast activity. It is called "fast," "paradoxical" or "dreaming" sleep, and it is thought that subcortical functions are then predominantly facilitated. Dreaming sleep recurs at intervals of about ninety minutes. There are rapid eye movements (REM) during dreaming. Respiration is irregular, heart rate and blood pressure are elevated, skin resistance is lowered, penile erection occurs, and there is rapid and distinctive diminution in muscle tone. Vocalization and facial activity occur only during dreaming.

"Deprivation of REM sleep by awakening establishes a deficit which must be made up in subsequent sleep periods and may be associated with psychopathology."[3] At least it appears that dreaming sleep may represent a physiological state that is significant in maintaining the psychological homeostasis of the individual. (Higher animals dream, also.) It has been suggested that the so-called toxic effects of drugs such as the amphetamines are due to the fact that they suppress this, the REM portion of the sleep cycle.[4]

Continuous lack of sleep produces deterioration in personality functioning, whether due solely to lack of sleep with the associated neuromuscular fatigue or even to the associated dream deprivation is not known.[5] The usually stated psychological changes are impairment of memory, irritability, difficulty in paying attention, hallucinations and illusions.

EXPERIMENTS WITH SLEEP

So many "so-called" experiments of sleep deprivation have been reported, from observing the behavior of participants in no-sleep marathons which have kept people awake for days, to watching good friends go to pieces and fight each other when deprived of sleep for more than twenty-four hours, that truly scientific experiments are to be welcomed.

One reported in the *Journal of Experimental Psychology*[6] was not particularly traumatizing or exciting, but is very informative. It investigated characteristic experiences of individuals under quite ordinary stress. Twenty-four young adult normal subjects were deprived of sleep from 7:00 a.m. Monday to 5:00 p.m. Tuesday (thirty-four hours). During the night they amused themselves in a recreation room; therefore, they were not harried or under strain; they were just awake. During the days they followed their usual routines or participated in being tested. After the end of the enforced wakefulness they were free to sleep until called at the usual time (6:30) Wednesday morning. The usual practice was to sleep for about two hours in the early evening, Tuesday, and to then remain awake until about 11:00 p.m., or their usual retiring time, that night.

The report of the experiment stated that tasks known to be particularly sensitive to the direct effects of sleep deprivation were still impaired on the day following restorative sleep. In other words, a normal night's sleep does not restore the moderately sleep deprived person to normal. It appeared, in this experiment, that the adverse influence of the aftereffect was less in the afternoon than in the morning, and this was interpreted as meaning that normal physiological rhythms were disturbed in the morning, due perhaps to the deeper or more prolonged restorative sleep the night before, and became partially re-established by the afternoon. The experimenter went on to conjecture that it may be that, when sleep has been lost, an aftereffect is best avoided by resuming normal routines as quickly as possible.

Scientists who have studied sleep have made other suggestions to guide the individual who desires sleep, as well as the social planner. It is agreed that rhythms of sleep are upset by rotating work shifts, by airplane travel which jumps time zones, and by the irregular living which is possible and so popular today, when electric light makes the rhythm of the earth in respect to the sun so unimportant for man's daily routine. Furthermore, the frequent impairment of sleep by the noise associated with modern civilization (automobiles, trucks, railways, jets) behooves city builders and traffic engineers to "take into consideration the need and right of every human to rest, a factor indispensable for health."[7]

In an effort to induce sleep for therapeutic purposes, as well as for experiments to study the characteristics of sleep and wakefulness, several methods have been used. In spite of the acknowledged dangers of constant recumbency for normal subjects,[8] a body of information has grown up favoring the use of sleep and relaxation in the recumbent position for a great many maladies.

The first extended use of the "rest cure" in the United States was in the practice of S. Weir Mitchell, in the late 19th century. Pierre Janet[9] also subscribed to rest of the body for treatment of the mind. He said that physicians always do well to prescribe rest in bed for a while. And Freud himself, who is remembered more for other ideas than for his bio-neurogenic explanation of neurasthenia, believed that it revealed marked similarities to conditions in those diseases which originate through the chronic influence of foreign poisons as well as through their acute diminution.[10] He believed that the symptoms of neurasthenia "must be regarded as direct toxic consequences of disturbed chemical processes."[11]

INFLUENCE OF PAVLOV ON STUDIES WITH SLEEP

Pavlov, when his turn came, also subscribed to a bio-psychological explanation of behavior. All these scholars and physicians undergirded the more recent psychosomatic explanation of human normalcy and pathology.[12]

Pavlov's teachings have had considerable influence on the development of sleep as therapy. As suggested previously in this chapter, he recognized sleep as an inhibition which protects the cells of the cortex from countless external stimuli and enables them to preserve a residue of vital activity. He believed that protective inhibition, in addition, in the form of sleep, can result in restoration of the normal cortical cell composition after it has been threatened or weakened.[13]

METHODS USED TO INDUCE SLEEP

Beyond general rest and sleep, which cannot be precisely dosed or controlled, physicians have had to prescribe other measures. Everyone is aware of the effectiveness of the age-long use of alcohol, and narcotics like opium to put the individual out of touch with reality and therefore out of mental control. But these means have varying effects on individuals and so are not precise enough for pre-scriptive purposes. When anesthetic drugs, which could be given orally, rectally or by injection, were available, they could and were used to induce sleep for therapeutic purposes. The barbiturates were used by general practitioners and even by specialists in psychi-atry who learned that direct and indirect psychotherapy could be especially effective as the patient came out from under the effects of the drug. Sleep therapy became "an accessory method creating a suitable background for deep therapy."[14] It proved to be most effective when used with subsequent active psychotherapy. It be-came known, to psychiatrists, as a particular stage in treatment, to prepare the nervous system for receiving subsequent forms of therapy.

But there are secondary effects of the barbiturates,[15] and gradually the tranquilizers have taken their place. But even these drugs are to be criticized. All drugs are toxic in some degree and electric anesthesia or electronarcosis is the modality which has attracted most attention recently for inducing sleep. It is based on Pavlov's teaching on the medical role of protective inhibition, and on the use of electricity in the institute in Russia named for him. There they began to avoid using large doses of drugs while Pavlov was still alive because of the development of unaccustomed and distressing sensations which impeded recovery. They wanted to induce sleep in a form approximating the physiological. Their aim was the use of proper influences to strengthen natural protective inhibition.

It may be difficult to accept the fact that electric current through the brain is less dangerous than drugs; but, when administered by a physician or authorized technician, it is not unpleasant and has no side effects. It is so subtle a modality that it can even be on or off in an experiment, and the subject not know the difference.

For example, it was used in these two ways in an initial experiment in India, reported in the International Journal of Neuropsychiatry.[16] The machine used was manufactured by the Moscow-Works of Electrical Medical Equipment and named "Portable Electric Sleep Apparatus." Two negative electrodes are to be applied on the closed eyelids and two positive electrodes on the mastoids. (On the sleep center side of the picture, the procedure of directing current from cathodes over the orbits to anodes placed on the mastoid processes, and having the current cross enroute, could strike the sleep waking centers of the hypothalamus[17] or reticular formation.) In the experiment here reported trials were carried out on 15 cases of anxiety state at an army hospital and 15 normal subjects (male nursing assistants). The duration of each electrosleep treatment varied from one and a half hours to two hours. The patients and subjects alike were told that the machine had been used in other countries, that it was not meant for giving electric shock, that very low voltage of current would be used, and that no harm could possibly come to him. The subject was asked to say if he felt any discomfort as the voltage was being gradually increased. The discomfort usually was described as a "pricking" and/or "burning sensation" in the eyes. This discomfort disappeared in all cases as the voltage was slightly reduced. The voltage used ranged from 5 to 20 volts (at 0.05 to 0.2 milliamperes). In this experiment 73.3 per cent of the patients and 26.6 per cent of the normal volunteers slept on one or more occasions.

Since it is possible, as Kleitman has suggested,[18] that the sleep which may follow the application of the current with this kind of machine may be the result of suggestion alone, 13 of the former 15 patients had the voltage reduced to zero during three sessions each, after he felt some discomfort with the increase in the voltage. In other words no current was going to the patient although he was unaware of this fact. The proportion of sleep per session for these trials was 15 per cent, which is not significantly different than the 13 per cent for the normal control group of 15 volunteers.

It can be assumed that, although current is passing through the brain when this machine is used, when the electrodes are applied as intended, the current is not uncomfortable in any worrisome way.

Although they have called their treatments "sleep therapy," physicians who have used electronarcosis elsewhere have not been as concerned as the Indian physicians as to whether or not their patients and subjects have slept during or immediately after the treatments or experiments. They have been grateful that it has not induced the side-effects due to sedatives.[19]

From the Institute of Therapy in the Academy of Medical Sciences, in Moscow, it has been reported that after 5 to 7 procedures, in courses of treatments involving daily sessions of thirty minutes to two hours from 11:00 a.m. to 1:00 p.m. after breakfast, with electrodes applied as described above, the duration of nocturnal sleep became longer, finally lasting eight to twelve hours; and the patients felt better the next morning. They even felt a desire to sleep from 11 to 1 on Sundays, during their courses of treatment, suggesting that the treatment sessions developed a conditioned or habit pattern.

SLEEP IN TREATMENT

The types of disorders for which sleep therapy, induced by drugs or by electronarcosis, has been used effectively are many, as various as myocardial infarction, essential hypertension, asthma, emphysema, gastric ulcer, disorders of the genitourinary tract, and in psychiatry except for obsessive compulsive reactions and "psychopathic states." It has been used after painful dental procedures, and before major surgery. The results appear to be due to effects on the brain and to psychological reactions from suggestion and monotony and comfort, or to both. The procedure has come to be less and less continuous and of shorter duration in total time as well as on each day. The treatments usually extend over several days, from seven to seventeen or eighteen, but sleep itself is interrupted several times, usually three each day, to allow for diversion, direct therapy, feeding, bathing, etc. Electro-sleep is light, transient, often refreshing, and sometimes accompanied by dreams.[20]

IN PSYCHIATRY

More use has been made of sleep therapy in psychotherapy than in any other branch of medicine. The best therapeutic results from sleep have been attained in neurasthenia, especially for patients with asthenic symptomatology. Possibly sleep therapy may be considered only as "an accessory method creating a suitable background for deep therapy."[21] It may be used as a particular stage in treatment, to prepare the nervous system for receiving subsequent forms of therapy. I am not a physician but have used relaxation techniques for patients referred to me by physicians. I can attest that deep relaxation does put a patient into a state that may be called extremely cooperative. He is then likely to spill out a great deal of repressed material, to become strongly dependent on the therapist, to "transfer" emotions readily, and to feel very appreciative of the help offered. It is because of these facts that some years ago, I decided never to serve another patient singly and to work only in groups where transference could be handled more safely and insight would spread for the benefit of more individuals. The psychological benefits of sleep therapy and of all other relaxation techniques probably reside in the same mechanisms.

The "suggestive" value of sleep therapy has been recognized by many practitioners and there is no reason to deprecate electronarcosis, as the Indian experimenters did, because true sleep did not always result during its application. Even they admit that the fear of inability to get proper sleep and the anticipatory anxiety connected therewith had resulted in disturbed sleep which had been very bothersome to the patient. Of course even the suggestion of inducing sleep for even a few hours is always an important therapeutic step. This applies also to all indications that relaxation may result from any measure, be it gentle massage, soothing heat, enjoyable music, repetititve sensory stimuli like the sound of a clock, or the quieting tone of a beloved and trusted voice.

It may be conjectured that there has been some prior loss of sleep for all patients who are benefited by sleep therapy, and that they crave sleep because they are afraid of insomnia. The depressed patient, particularly, finds insomnia to be the most unpleasant of his symptoms. "Primary" insomnia, implying unknown causality, may reflect hereditary predisposition of constitution and temperament. "Secondary" insomnia implies various organic and psychic circumstances which raise the threshold of wakefulness.[22] Be this as it may, anything which offers a relief from insomnia is sure to be welcomed and usually to be participated in whole-heartedly when it is sought or agreed to. When one admits how much importance the ordinary mortal attaches to a few hours of sleep at regular intervals, one can imagine how distressing insomnia will make a nervous individual.

Sleep therapy seems to have carved a large niche for itself in psychiatry and psychosomatic medicine. Even patients with severe mental disturbance, involving anxiety, depression, conversion headaches and neuromuscular tension, who are severely insomniac and refractory to other therapy, have responded favorably to all forms of sleep therapy, particularly electro-sleep. The results reported in *The Sciences,* published under the auspices of the New York Academy of Medicine,[23] are acknowledged to be due to physical changes in the body economy and not merely to suggestion. It is to be admitted, of course, that psychiatrists welcome and seek sleep because emotionally charged material can be better handled when the patient is rested after a good sleep.[24]

Many truly scientific experiments have been carried out with sleep, for neuro-psychiatric patients, with proper controls. To discuss any number of them in detail would seem to be extraneous at this juncture, since new ones are being undertaken in all countries with advanced medical technology and are reported in the popular as well as scientific press. Evaluation of the effectiveness of sleep therapy has been undertaken by simple tabulation of sleep induction during treatment, by verbal responses regarding the quality of subsequent nocturnal sleep and rest, by noting how many sessions were needed, by changes in pulse and respiration rates, which of course are evidence of physical changes in the body economy, and by other behavioral alterations. Attainment of sleep during treatment, as looked for in the Indian experiment reported above, has by no means been given priority in all the experiments, but instead the getting of a good night's sleep afterward and in the discontinuance of the use of drugs during the night hours as quickly as possible. It is to be reported that beneficial effects of the therapy investigated in these experiments has extended in a secondary way into other areas of improvement such as betterment of interpersonal relationships and increased productiveness as well as raised thresholds of withstanding the stresses and conflicts of everyday living.

Sleep therapy has not been credited for bringing about real "cures" with truly psychotic patients or with those having personality disorders of long standing; but lessening of suffering for all concerned has been noted. As wise observers have said, "one improved (if not recovered) psychiatric patient is a 100 per cent statistic for that patient and his family."[25]

It is acknowledged, in psychiatry, that overfatigue, chronic lack of sleep, infections and other irritants weaken the nervous system so that the slightest psychogenic factor (social or familial) can produce a neurosis; or "a complicated situation of conflict can operate for a long time without producing a disease, but the addition of any (somatic) factor may provoke a neurotic reaction to preexisting difficulties."[26] This statement should cover considerations of psychosomatic disorders. So many pathological conditions resemble those induced by fatigue that it has been logical, of course, to presuppose that rest and sleep will favor improvement. But controlled experiments with sleep-therapy have confirmed this hypothesis. In one to be cited, the doctors found support for their feeling that psychosomatic illness represents a "masked depression."[27]

"The period of prolonged narcosis was of fourteen days' duration, with the patients asleep except for three wake periods per twenty-four hours. . . . The medications were started on the night of the fifth day after admission and thereafter were given with breakfast, lunch and at 9:00 p.m. . . . The patients were awakened early in the morning, around noon, and at 6:00 p.m. so that they could take their meals, undertake mild exercise and be seen by their physicians for physical examinations and interviews. . . . All patients readily regressed within three to four days after the onset of drug-induced prolonged narcosis . . . and experienced euphoria with a general sense of well-being and disappearance of somatic symptoms. . . . All patients demonstrated marked dependency early in regression and made extensive demands on the nursing staff. . . . Following gradual discontinuation of sleep medication, all patients continued to show absence of their original physical symptoms. . . . The results (of the experiment) indicate that the basic personality structure of the patients had not changed, but there were definite changes in the ways the patients were able to express themselves. . . . They were free of somatic complaints, relieved of anxiety, and their sleep patterns had changed from a depressed pattern into a pattern considered normal."

The results of the experiment were that, "in a Pavlovian sense, sleep therapy can be seen to be effective by giving the target organ a rest . . . (and) that sleep therapy per se can produce remission in psychosomatic illness, but that psychotherapy at the termination of the regressive period is necessary to provide best improvement." The orientation for this experiment was definitely psychiatric.

Some investigations with sleep as therapy have not been weighted as heavily toward psychotherapy. As Cabot suggested, emotions are responsible for bodily disturbances, but so also are overwork and physical stress; and sleep reaches both. In sleep we not only rest, but escape immediate emotion and ventilate, in dreams, our past emotions. Dreaming sleep is now acknowledged to represent a physiological drive state that is significant in maintaining the psychological homeostasis of the organism.[28] Maybe dreaming does the trick. At least it can be said that continuous lack of sleep definitely produces deterioration in bodily as well as personality functioning, whether due solely to lack of sleep, to dream deprivation, or to associated muscular fatigue is not known.

IN HEART DISEASE AND CIRCULATORY DISTURBANCES

There are some physical disorders which are not thought of as psychogenic exclusively or even particularly—the circulatory disorders, for example. They, too, have responded favorably to sleep therapy. Acute myocardial infarction surely has precise physical manifestations, although the pain and fear which accompany the attacks may predispose to cardiac arrest. At Charing Cross Hospital in London, 59 acute myocardial infarction patients, in age from thirty-seven to seventy-eight, were put in light sleep for one to seven days by drugs,[29] in an intensive care unit. There was only one death, during the sleep regimen, and that was due to gastrointestinal hemorrhage. The patients were returned to general wards three to five days after treatment. Only 8 died there after the intensive care.

The expected mortality of patients with acute myocardial infarction is about 50 per cent from arrhythmias at the onset of illness. The causes of death in the general wards after sleep therapy were various.

The regimen in intensive care allowed the patients to be wakened three times daily for feeding, washing and physical therapy. It was continued until, upon arousal, the patient looked well and rested, and was free from agitation, pain, hypotension and impairment of peripheral circulation or arrhythmia. The average length of sleep treatment to satisfy the physicians was two and one half days, for their main purpose was to reduce the pain and mental stress during the period of greatest risk, the first few days after the initial attack. They reported that, although future tests may not support the impression that sleep plays a vital and beneficial role in the treatment of myocardial infarction, they are satisfied that this approach seems to provide the patient with the most pleasant introduction to life with cardiac damage

IN INTERNAL MEDICINE IN GENERAL

In internal medicine sleep induction has had many other applications. It has been used for treating gastric ulcer, asthma and emphysema as well as hypertension and post-acute myocardial infarction. "In surgery, it has been used to reduce anxiety by inducing sleep on the ward prior to departure for the operating room. A combination of electrosleep and a local anesthetic in minor surgery permits physicians to reduce greatly the dosage of anesthetic drugs."[30] Electro-narcosis has even been used, in the form of electric anesthesia, in major surgery.

RELAXATION IN CONNECTION WITH DENTISTRY

This brings us to a discussion of relaxation per se, without sleep, in two fields close to medicine—dentistry and childbirth. Some dentists claim that extreme tension even influences periodontal disease, possibly because the mouth is directly or symbolically related to all so-called human passions. Emotions may not directly cause disease, of course, but they are credited with setting the stage for disease processes. Bottled up tensions and anxieties, and the same expressed in nail biting and gnashing of the teeth, have a direct effect on periodontal tissues by traumatic shunting of teeth.

Other dentists introduce a relaxing atmosphere in their offices through the use of music and pleasing decor, and study psychology to influence their patients, knowing that thereby they can reduce pain and anxiety before they must induce pain or use fear producing instruments. These are usual procedures in dentistry.

Recently a more subtle relation of tension to dental disease has been intimated. Dentists are indicting the public for the too general use of tranquilizing drugs. "Mouth dryness" is a common side effect of such drugs and increases the impulse to smoke more. Then the soft tissues of the mouth become more susceptible to disease and the teeth more prone to decay.[31]

RELAXATION IN PREPARATION FOR CHILDBIRTH

Smoking, which accompanies nervousness and, therefore, the use of tranquilizers, has also been indicated in relation to childbearing. But there is more need for relaxation techniques in childbearing than just as a modality preferred to tranquilizing drugs. The greatest hazard of pregnancy is fear of pain, combined with a sense of personal inadequacy. Fear and worry help to create pain, and make the process of childbearing just what it is not intended to be—a harrowing experience.[32]

It may not be appropriate to go into a complete routine for training a woman during her antenatal period; but I have had extensive experience, not only with brides in school and college but with private and clinic patients in a large maternity hospital.*

It should be sufficient here to say just a few words about justifications for and patterns of relaxation techniques, and to refer to the fuller discussion of preparation for childbirth in the reference cited immediately above. Perhaps it will not be most comfortable to relax flat on the back when one is pregnant, but the essential method of training oneself to release any excess tension in the various regions of the body can be practiced in any posture in which the body is

* Wesson Maternity Hospital, Springfield, Massachusetts.

being supported. Remember that when any part of the body relaxes the whole is benefited. In relation to pregnancy, and even for
the first stage of labor, a rest position which has been suggested is on
one side with the under arm placed behind the trunk. The arm on
top should be placed in a half bent position on the bed in front. The
under leg should be bent slightly and the upper leg should be bent
still more, with the knee placed well in front, on a pillow for comfort.
This is the position in which a woman can rest between childbirth
contractions, during the first stage of labor particularly. The first
stage is the period during which the sphincter is relaxing and the
uterine wall is retracting to open the cervix. Surely no extra contraction of the abdominal wall or diaphragm is expected during this
stage. Relaxation is entirely in order then. The second stage begins, usually, when the labor contractions are spaced at about two-
minute intervals. In these intervals, relaxation is also desirable.
During the contractions the woman may be permitted to push to
help the baby through the birth canal, but otherwise she should be
in a tranquil state and as fully relaxed as possible.

So we come to the end of this discussion of sleep and relaxation
techniques in therapy, with no mention of the methods which may
be most important of all—unconditioned and conditioned reflex
sleep. That is left for the final chapter, when the ultimate devices
of self-control and self-management are explained.

REFERENCES

1. Mitchell, S. Weir. *Fat and Blood:* An Essay on the Treatment of Certain
   Forms of Neurasthenia and Hysteria, 4th ed., Philadelphia: J. B. Lippin-
   cott Co., 1885.
2. *The Anatomy of Sleep*, Roche Laboratories, Div. of Hoffman-LaRoche, Inc.,
   Nutley, N. J., 1966, p. 56.
3. Kolb, Lawrence C. *Noyes Modern Clinical Psychiatry*, 7th ed., Philadelphia:
   W. B. Saunders Co., 1968, p. 27.
4. Ibid., p. 13.
5. Ibid., p. 126.
6. Wilkinson, Robert T. *Aftereffect of Sleep Deprivation*, Jour. of Exp. Psych.,
   66:5:439–442 (November) 1963.
7. Richter, H. R. *The EEG and the impairment of sleep by traffic noise during the
   night, a problem of preventive medicine.* Electroenceph. clin. Neurophysiol. *23*:
   291 (September) 1967.

8. Leithauser, Daniel J. *Early Ambulation and Related Procedures in Surgical Management*, Springfield: Charles C Thomas, 1946.
9. Janet, Pierre. *Psychological Healing*, New York: The Macmillan Co., 1925, Vol. 1, Chap. 9. Treatment by Rest, pp. 372–484; Vol. 2, Chap. 15, Psychophysiological Methods of Treatment, pp. 1030–1077.
10. Freud, Sigmund. *A General Introduction to Psychoanalysis*, 17th ed., New York: Boni & Liveright, 1927.
11. Freud, Sigmund. *An Autobiographical Study*, The Problem of Lay-Analysis, New York: Brentanos, 1927.
12. Dunbar, H. Flanders. *Mind and Body: Psychosomatic Medicine*, Rev. ed., New York: Random House, 1955.
13. Williams, Robert L. & Wilse B. Webb. *Sleep Therapy*, Springfield: Charles C Thomas, 1966.
14. Andreev, B. V. *Sleep Therapy in the Neuroses*, New York: Consultants Bureau, 1960. Translated from Russian by Basil Haigh.
15. Hartman, Ernest. *Dauerschlaf: A Polygraphic Study*, Arch. Gen. Psychiatry, *18*:99–111, 1968.
16. Singh, K. *Sleep Inducing Devices: A Clinical Trial with a Russian Machine*, Int. J. Neuropsychiat., *3*:311–18 (July-Aug.) 1967.
17. Long, Roy C. *Electrosleep Therapy*, Jour. Kansas Medical Society, Feb. 1966, pp. 81–85.
18. Kleitman, Nathaniel. *Sleep and Wakefulness*, Chicago: University of Chicago Press, Enlarged ed., 1963, p. 299.
19. Andreev, op. cit., p. 8.
20. Williams and Webb, op. cit., p. 26.
21. Andreev, op. cit., pp. 30 & 79.
22. The Anatomy of Sleep, op. cit., p. 97.
23. *Sleep Therapy*, The Sciences, published by the New York Academy of Sciences, *8*:7:33–37 (July) 1968.
24. Long, op. cit.
25. Williams and Webb, op. cit., p. 23.
26. Ibid., p. 14.
27. Marder, L. and J. D. Hoogerheets. *Regressive Sleep Therapy in the Treatment of Psychosomatic Disorders*, Psychosomatics, VIII:322–325 (Nov.-Dec.) 1967.
28. Kolb., op. cit., p. 130.
29. Nixon, P. G. F., D. J. E. Taylor, S. D. Morton and M. Bromfield. *A Sleep Regimen for Acute Myocardial Infarction*, The Lancet, (April 6) 1968, pp. 726–728.
30. *Sleep Therapy*, op. cit.
31. Protell, Martin R., D.D.S.: Reported at Meeting of N. Y. Dental Society, December, 1968.
32. Rathbone, Josephine L. and Valerie V. Hunt. *Corrective Physical Education*, Philadelphia; W. B. Saunders Co., 7th ed., 1965, p. 196 ff.
33. Ciba Foundation. Symposium on *The Nature of Sleep*, Boston: Little, Brown & Co., 1961. (Editors for the Foundation: G. E. W. Wolstenholme and Maeve O'Connor.)
34. Foulkes, David. *The Psychology of Sleep*, New York: Charles Scribner's Sons, 1966.

Power Over Oneself: Conscious Relaxing

MEANING OF SELF CONTROL

THE FIRST PART OF THE TITLE for the last chapter of this book on relaxation does not satisfy me. "Power" has been used instead of "control" because, through the years, students and audiences have reacted unfavorably to the suggestion that people who cannot relax at will do not have self-control. Perhaps self-management or self-direction would be acceptable to tense people who take themselves very seriously and who think they are exemplary, and therefore self-controlled. But "management" and "direction" do not connote doing those little things, each day, that should be done, and leaving undone those little things that should not be done. This is what tense people need.

As Edmund Jacobson says,* whereas man has made and is making successful studies of his environment, he has failed to make comparable strides toward increasing his own personal efficiency. Man needs self-engineering, which will result in his acquiring self-reliance. Self-reliance would be the reward of self-control.

The followers of Pavlov, who have had so much influence in sleep therapy, have used an idea which covers the one we shall try to get across in this chapter—unconditioned and conditioned reflex

* Jacobson, Edmund *et al.* *Tension in Medicine*, Springfield: Charles C Thomas, 1967.

relaxation. Individuals can look for features in their own environments which will inevitably lead to a state of relaxation; those will come under the heading of "unconditioned." They also can induce relaxation in themselves by habit formation; that will be "conditioned."

Of course, electro-narcosis cannot be available outside of institutions; and physicians, who have been interested in finding and in developing aids to relaxation and sleep, have been advocating less and less drugs and never self-medication. Therefore, it behooves everyone to listen to what scientists and therapists can say about measures which everyone can use. And, really, those are the only measures that can have any great influence over the common problems, in our society, of insomnia and "stress."

HYPNOSIS

Hypnosis is a measure that has been advocated for escape from tension and therefore for relaxation, ever since the days of Mesmer, but it also is open to serious criticism. In the first place, it must be induced artificially, or it necessitates the influence of another personality, to be true hypnosis. What is really meant by this term is a trance-like condition in which the subject is in a state of suggestibility. As actually seen in practice in psychiatrists' offices and in classrooms, where the purpose of what is called "hypnosis" is to put the subject into a state of physical relaxation or sleep, the results, when successful, are absolutely no different from what a person can achieve in a physical education class, in a group therapy session, or in his own home, by the use of methods suggested in Chapters 5 and 6 in this book.

In reverse, the methods advocated in this book have been called hypnotic by people who do not know what true hypnosis is. To be sure, when a teacher or therapist is helping a subject or patient to learn how to relax it may look, to an observer, as though the subject or patient were under the power of the teacher or therapist. But that is to be deplored, if ever true. The purpose of the relaxation techniques herein advocated is to make it possible for the subject or patient to relax himself, to be under his own control.

And that is not self-hypnosis, either. It is just having the results follow the practice of a skill or routine which works, not a suggestion.

Hypnotism can work only when the subject believes it can do so, when he puts his faith in the hypnotist. When people put faith in their doctors, ministers, teachers or friends, what they have to offer can also "work." In this sense what one can do for oneself will also "work" if one has faith in oneself. This is the most important element in guiding oneself into a state of relaxation, to have some skills which will inevitably "work" so one can trust them and trust himself.

CONSCIOUS RELAXING

The second part of the title of this chapter—conscious relaxing, which is just the opposite of being hypnotized—does satisfy me. It is a term I began to use forty years ago. I then was aware that the people who needed help most were brilliant—the best students in my classes, and the most scholarly of my professional colleagues. When I went to the Far East, a decade later, in search for an explanation of the statement, in medical literature, that hypertensive disease was not to be found in the hospitals of India and China, I discovered that scholars there bit their nails before examinations as they do here, and professional people there came to me for advice when someone told them that I had written a dissertation on neuromuscular hypertension. People with hypertensive disease were not in hospital clinics because they were in the "upper" class, which did not use hospitals, and because those institutions served the poor people in the study of such diseases as filiariasis and malaria, and for the treatment of "Peking fever," suppurating sores, etc. Relaxing, conscious or otherwise, was not their need.

Surely highly intelligent people should be able to learn how to relax, when they can learn other skills so easily. The difficulty is that they really do not want to learn to relax. They like the satisfactions which come from their activities. If they have ever been threatened by an illness which they associate with hypertension, or if they have become nearly "crazy" with insomnia, and if they hear of a therapist who can "perform miracles" they may go to him;

but unless he gives them a whopping big bill in advance of his treatments they will probably not do as he advises. They have to want to relax more than they want anything else to follow suggestions which call for changes of behavior on their own part. Drugs are easy to take, but self-management and doing simple things, like those described in Chapter 5, are very difficult indeed for an individual who cannot marshal his will for his own good. That's what is meant by not having self-control.

ESCAPE INTO DRUGS

Some drugs, of course, have their place for many diseases, and to reach the physical basis of some behavior. If we criticize soporific and hallucinatory drugs in this chapter, it is not for moral reasons. That people should turn to such drugs in emergencies or in curiosity is not strange, but why they do so, in excess, is a puzzlement to anyone who has been willing to meet life's difficulties, not escape them. However, we should not moralize. The causes of anxieties in our modern world should need no reciting. That some people are easily frustrated and flattened by anxieties may not be understandable to those whose "thresholds" are so high that they can continue to live with them without stress (see p. 4f). But they must beware: they too may be floored if the blows they receive are too hard or if they are weakened by environmental or personal traumas.

There is no reason for us to discuss at length such modern escape devices as marihuana and LSD. They definitely do have serious side effects, however. They are more potent than alcohol, which has been imbibed all over the world, as long as man has wanted to forget his woes or to be happier and more sociable. Furthermore, they are more difficult to "sleep off." They are of interest here because their use may reflect more acute maladjustments of today.

NEEDS OF YOUNG PEOPLE

A moderate use of alcohol has been acceptable socially and even can be prescribed medically, for relaxing purposes; but everyone— layman or physician—is afraid of hallucinatory drugs. Perhaps

11

what we are really afraid of are the conditions, in the lives of modern adolescents especially, which induce them to behave in ways that puzzle us, and to want these drugs. We do not like the boys' long hair nor the dishevelled appearance of so many young people. We call them dirty. We criticize them for their apparent vacuity and unproductiveness. We are worried because they will not accept our advice about their conduct or their friends.

In that regard are they any different than we were at their age? Are they just better organized to express their dissatisfactions with the status quo? And do they have a vocabulary that we do not understand? Because we are as established as we shall ever be, and are conforming to patterns of conduct much the same as our parents accepted, and theirs before them, the young people of today call us "the establishment." And they openly criticize us. They feel sure they can do better than we, their predecessors, have done. God help them!

Many young people from homes of privilege, today, are opposed to the hypocrisy they sense in those homes and the empty marriages in the families they know, to the dullness and mediocrity they see all about them, and to the human rat-race in general. They admit to being bored and discontented because they want something better. They feel lonely and unloved, not by their own parents necessarily, but by their nation, which sends the boys away to be killed and leaves the girls at home without boyfriends and possibly never to have husbands. They are rebellious, and rightly so.

The "have not" young people are rebellious also. What does life hold for them? They may want the glitter that the other young people see as tawdry, and they are more insecure than the others because they identify with their people, who have not been able to give them any material advantages. They are not in rebellion against a previous generation of "have nots" but against the same group as the other young people—against the "establishment."

These two groups of young people are coming closer and closer together. In their rebellions they are not distrusting each other as much as those who already have jobs—the general membership of the labor unions and the captains of industry—still distrust each other. In their dress there is no separatism; together they have adopted the flowing robes of gurus of India and the amulets and headdresses of American Indians.

RETURN TO RELIGIONS

There is a return together, on the part of young people, to religious precepts of the past. Just as the young chiefs of the Indian tribes of America, who have served their new nation in its battles, are returning to the hogans and kivas of their ancestors in disdain, so the Negroes are seeking guidance from the Islam of their Muslim past, the Jewish young people are fascinated by Israel, and the white European-American Christians are struggling to find a faith to which they can subscribe, based on the fundamental teachings of Jesus instead of the external trappings of formalized church organizations and dogma. All these young people are seeking some support from their pasts, to be sure, and yet some guidance into the future from Gods they think are loving. They are crying out for love.

SEEKING FOR LOVE

When one reads the statements made by representatives of these young people, and when one learns of a huge rally of Hindus and Christians in London's biggest cathedral to honor the memory of Gandhi, one is impressed with the emphasis placed on love and on simple goodness. Whereas their forebears made fun of Mahatma Gandhi, they—Christians and Hindus—join in worshipping at his shrine of love.

There is joy in the love they talk about, even those of the younger generation whose malaise and apathy have driven them toward hallucinogenic drugs. Even they have found a new religion, they believe. It lacks a substantial base, to be sure, but it expresses the need of all of them who are trying to escape this mundane and unsatisfying existence. The religion which accompanies hallucinogenic drugs does not come from within man but, instead, from the drugs which are applied to man from the outside. But the fact that our young people, who are most disturbed—the ones seeking psychodelic escapes—are welcoming any God, even of their own making, is telling us how the past generations have failed in developing a comforting, meaningful religion, and how young people, in deep distress, think they can do better. Maybe they can, but not by using drugs when they are out of control. They can only do so by seeking goodness, kindess and mastery of themselves.

SIMPLE SUGGESTIONS FOR ALL

Whether or not the suggestions to follow in this chapter can be of any help, to those who are so distraught and confused as to use drugs, cannot be foreseen. What is sure, however, is that they can help those who still want to share the good life, as we know it, with others who do not use drugs and who desire to build creatively for a better life. Possibly, also, these suggestions will alert adults, who know what tension has brought into their own lives, to appeal to teachers, ministers and public officials like prosecutors and law officers to get more involved, with information media, in education about the dangers of drug abuse before it leads to decay of our culture as well as individual young people.

These young people are seeking physical as well as spiritual help from less mechanized and material centered cultures than our own. They have gone to India to study with gurus who have become skilled in the âsanas (postures) and pranayamas (breathing techniques) of Hatha (physical) Yoga. They have learned, here at home, that the only way to keep a person awake without stimulating drugs (for they have played with them also) is to use his muscles, by dancing, walking, talking, even by talking to himself; so they have understood that a way to shut off consciousness would be to stop using the muscles, to relax. They have gone to India to learn a physical or exercise way which they understand leads to spiritual quiet and peace. If they could be given faith in other suggestions like those in Chapter 5 some of them would try those.

They have tried comfort here at home, in loose clothes, as they have in India. Some of them have also used soothing massage and other means to reduce pain without drugs. Some of them have learned that a small range of temperature change, of 1 to 2 degrees, will further relaxation. That is about the amount that is influenced by exercise and the surcease thereof. One should realize that body temperature decreases in sleep and that it is better to be a little cool at night, for the most restful sleep.

Repetitious sensory stimulation is also relaxing. Are not dentists' offices and industrial plants and supermarkets equipped with "canned" music, to calm patients and employees, and to encourage buying and to discourage brigandage? It has been learned that the best use of music in work situations, where people must remain for several hours, is not continuous but for an hour or so in the A.M. and again in the P.M., It should be a combination of classical or "worth hearing again" and popular selections.

Other repetitious sensory stimuli, which calm the spirit and can even bore the brain to give up its battle with facts and wakefulness, are the sound of a clock or air conditioner and the rhythmic flashing of lights, as any urban dweller knows who has difficulty going to sleep on the first few nights of his vacation in the country. Also the monotony of a droning lecturer will bore the brain, as all students know. This can be carried over into listening to a loved voice at bedtime, in order to sink into greatly desired sleep.

NEED FOR CONFIDENCE

Personal rituals, like those mentioned above, which can be introduced at bedtime will invariably work, if the subject has faith in them. Just as the doctor, who is sought by a patient close to breakdown, assures that patient that some hypnotic will work and then gives him a sufficiently large dose of a drug to be sure of producing an effect for a few nights, so the teacher who recommends a ritual or gadget or panacea to gradually condition sleep must surround it with an aura to make it inevitably effective. The teacher must be trusted as is the physician. This is the difficult part, and explains one reason why books like this are written—to give other teachers status, and assure readers that their ideas are founded on sound principles.

One recommendation that really is true, and is flattering to the one who receives it, is that the fierce rate of mental activity must be slowed before going to bed. It is true, as mentioned frequently in this text, that the highly intellectual mental worker is the one who finds it hardest to relax. The man who is all tensed up, biting his nails, twitching in his chair, fighting his telephone, will spend more physical energy than he is given credit for; and the dame who must keep the numerous committees in her ladies' organization working, her house clean and her childern in competition with her neighbors' "brats" will not be able to fall asleep at night, no matter how tired she feels.

COUNTERACTING INSOMNIA

Perhaps the most effective way to end this book is to concentrate on some ways to help these sufferers, for they are just that, to condition good patterns for inducing sleep. As has been mentioned before, lack of ability to sleep readily and soundly, and whenever desired, is the most common complaint of tense people. Some spend fortunes in efforts to regain the ability to sleep as well as they could in infancy. Others, less wealthy, just go fussing alone, trying all types of self-medication to no avail. Insomnia never killed a man unless it destroyed his sanity and let his worries so prey upon his mind that he took his own life. People just cannot bear staying awake all the time, however. They crave sleep for forgetfulness, if not for physical recuperation.

Insomnia is always accompanied by a sense of residual tension and can always be overcome when one successfully ceases to contract the parts of the body involved. In all insomnia it is possible for the sufferer to recognize a definite degree of tension in some muscles. This sensation of tension may even be present in the morning upon waking, and indicate to the individual that he has not been relaxed even in his sleep, as is quite possible.

To summarize what has been said about insomnia in the previous chapters, sleep is a psychophysical condition which usually occurs rhythmically, but which can be delayed by either physical or psychological factors. There are people who sleep without very great need for rest, and there are others, with great need for rest and recuperation, who cannot sleep. It is when one is too tense that sleep evades.

The mind is a psychophysical mechanism conditioned by habits. The only way to discipline it is to modify its habit patterns. It has been observed that for tense people of all ages the habit patterns of their minds and the resulting sleeplessness are to be explained by one of two "mind sets." Either they do not want to sleep or they are afraid to sleep.

The insomniacs who belong in the first category are the self-sufficient individuals who think that it is a waste of time to shut off the power of the mind. A poignant story is that of a college student who could not be influenced to adopt a sensible sleep routine. She knew her body was not very strong, but she was convinced that her mind could be dynamic and continuously creative without the support of healthful procedures. She held a very high academic rank throughout four college years, she supported herself by odd jobs; she slept very irregularly and very sparingly. She died, less than two years after graduation, of a disease that finds a ready medium in young people like herself—tuberculosis.

The insomniacs who are afraid to sleep are more numerous than one would suppose. Many of them were conditioned to poor sleep habits in childhood. Just delve back into the memories of your own childhood for moments when you listened for the retreating or returning footsteps of your mother, for you did not trust the servant or baby sitter; or recreate those episodes when you, as an older child, were left to guard the castle from robbers, fire, and pestilence. You had been taught prayers to sustain you. But such prayers!

> "Now I lay me down to sleep,
> I pray the Lord my soul to keep.
> And if I die before I wake,
> I pray the Lord my soul to take."

Great comfort for a child who otherwise would have no thought of death! How far from the essentials of a constructive plea like that expressed in the last verse of the 19th Psalm:

> "Let the words of my mouth, and the meditation of my heart, be acceptable in thy sight, Oh Lord, my strength and my redeemer."

What a mistake to put into anyone's mind thoughts to disturb and confuse, when at eventide the mind should settle down into a peace and quiet which encourages trustful rest and blissful sleep!

As we go along through the years we should try to remedy errors in training like those mentioned above. We should crowd out of consciousness, when the time for sleeping approaches, our forebodings of evil and our hates as well as petty grievances. Then we should let the cares of the day slip away.

SIMPLE TRICKS TO INDUCE SLEEP

Sleep time should not be serious thought time. It becomes absolutely imperative for a wakeful person to learn how to control his thought patterns, at least. No better way has been found to shut off all thought than the techniques of total relaxation discussed in Chapters 5 and 6. When the muscles of the gross body—the muscles which posture the body during mental work, and especially the finer muscles of the speech and reading mechanisms are relieved of tension, sleep inevitably follows. This technique never fails, but it is extremely hard to master. It is helpful, therefore, for a poor sleeper to learn some simple tricks to play on his unruly mind. Among the following, surely one will work. Habits are as hard to form as to break; so, if you select one trick as worth trying, put it into practice for at least ten consecutive nights before discarding it as useless. With ten tricks to try, you have more than three possible months of entertainment ahead. Before the three months have passed you will not be complaining of insomnia.

1. Prepare for sleep by cutting down on the intensity of your thinking for half an hour or more before retiring. For example, play a game of Chinese checkers. Write a letter to a friend, telling him of the pleasant things you have been doing.

2. Then take plenty of time to get ready for bed. Do not expect to leave your work or a heated discussion, in a state of exhilaration, and, tearing off your clothes and bouncing into bed, fall immediately into deep slumber. Get your clothes ready for the next morning, take a leisurely bath, brush your teeth especially well, and comb that thinning and graying hair. (How foolish these suggestions must ap-

pear to people who never have any difficulty falling to sleep. But neither these suggestions nor this book were written for them.)

3. Probably it is unwise to stimulate your mind in any way, if you are quite sleepless, but if you like to read in bed, choose non-fiction and a "hard" book. Force your mind to grapple with cumbersome facts; do not entertain it. Bore it into unconditional surrender to sleep. (For the person who is not troubled with insomnia on the other hand, no diversion is more satisfying than reading in a half-reclining position, in good light. For hard workers who wish to rest the body while "improving" the mind, no device is better than lying on a couch throughout a long evening, with a good book as companion and distant scenes as environment.)

4. Those who can concentrate best can sleep best. If your mind wants to cling to your fears or your hates, you must transplant it. Your mind cannot be in two places at once. The new field must hold interest but not excitement. Why not try planning a new wardrobe? Next season you must buy a new hat. Will a gray one or a blue one go better with your left-over suits? If you are going to buy a new suit or a new dress, what color will it be? Brown is going to be fashionable, but you look better in black or navy blue. What colors will you select for the accessories? On and on your mind can ramble and be wrenched back every time it wanders from this consciously selected track. If, as it wanders, it strikes upon an idea which may be useful tomorrow, jot down that idea on a pad kept, for just such an occasion, on a table at the side of the bed. Then discipline your mind to go directly back to the wardrobe planning.

You may prefer to divert your mind with some less frivolous theme, but never make the mistake of choosing one which is associated too closely with your occupation. You know the story of the suit and coat manufacturer who, in an effort to discipline his mind and woo sleep, through his imagination sheared 5,000 head of sheep, spun all the yarn himself, wove all the cloth, made it into good suits to sell for $39.95, took them to New York himself, and was forced to sell them at a loss of $5.50 per suit. He didn't sleep that night.

5. Have you noticed that, just as the mind loses consciousness and floats into sleep, thoughts become disjointed and scattered? Out of that phenomenon we can grab another technique for consciously in-

12 ⅄

ducing sleep. Make your mind hop from one idea to another. Start with some happy episode in childhood. Let it be when you made cider in the old meat-grinder on the back porch, with the juice dripping through the baby's gauze wash cloth into an old pail. Jack was there. He was the one who told you to throw in the rotten apples too. Beautiful Janet was there—the belle from Louisville, who loved to chew gum when her Granny could not see her. You wonder where Jack and Janet are now. Jack has married—whom— there was a baby—we must keep babies away from rat poison— Flit won't kill rats—there were cases and cases of Flit on the boat going out to Syria—the Mediterranean was so blue—red hair contrasts beautifully in a picture of ——. You are asleep.

These five suggestions for breaking poor sleeping habits have related particularly to control of the mind. The body is due some attention also. If it is calm, the mind cannot be very active.

1. The first technique to quiet the body is to get rid of any pain or pressure. Of course, a person who relaxes perfectly will not be inclined to feel a great deal of pain, since much pain is due to muscle tenseness as protection from motion. Pressure can be relieved on the surface of the body by removing shoes, loosening belts, making light the burden of covers at night. Discomfort from gas pressure or hyperactive stomach wall can sometimes be relieved by a very light snack.

(It seems appropriate to warn good relaxers, as well as those who have difficulty with this art, to check with a medical authority the cause of any troublesome pain or gastro-intestinal discomfort. If a physician suggests either heat or massage as a remedy, it should be applied by a very skilled technician. If he suggests a drug, it should be administered, but only when and in the exact amount he recommends. With heat, massage, and medicine, efforts should also be made to relax the part involved. When there is no distinct pain, it is doubtful whether heat, massage, or drugs should be used. Surely the only reason a sensible person would take a sleeping potion, for example, would be to upset a faulty habit pattern. He would take the drug for only one or two nights to help get a new habit pattern established.)

2. Better than extreme heat and less dangerous than drugs is a tepid bath just before retiring. This bath, however, should not be used after taking sleeping pills which may "work" when their user is in the tub and, therefore, cause him to commit suicide. The relaxing tepid bath should not be followed with a brisk rub-down. Instead, the body should be patted dry, so that one gets into bed a little damp and chilly. Then, as the surface is warmed, the whole body becomes more and more comfortable. If, during the night, one becomes sleepless, it is worth while to throw back the bedclothes, relieve the pressure in the bladder immediately, and get back into bed with the surface of the body possibly uncomfortably chilly. Then, when the covers are pulled up again, the body once more sinks into coziness and comfort.

3. Another purely physical technique to increase body comfort and induce complete relaxation is to practice some of the "breathing" exercises following p. 88, or to imitate the slow, deep, rhythmical breathing of sleep. It is entertaining and diverting to analyze one's rhythm of breathing, and some observers have credited controlled breathing with psychological rewards. Meditation is easier to achieve along with the sense of peacefulness and well-being that steals over one when breathing becomes slow, full, and rhythmic.

Controlled breathing, however, is effective as a relaxing device only as it stops flutterings and gaspings and the holding of breath. It really has no relation to the body's need for air. Oxygen need follows the muscles' need. When muscles are relaxed, they will need very little oxygen. Then, and then only, can the breathing be definitely slowed down and made more shallow. Ultimately rhythm and depth of breathing depend upon oxygen need.

4. To relax the muscles completely will induce sleep. Any time of day or night, if the muscles of the limbs, trunk, neck, and mask are relaxed, one will be unable to remain awake. Really, the most worth-while trick for inducing sleep is relaxing in the manner suggested on pages 91 to 103.

5. The last of the ten tips for inducing sleep may be the most important. Perhaps it should have been suggested first. It happens to be the most demanding, however, and only a very determined and

cooperative seeker after sleep will be inclined to select it. Yet, to his great satisfaction, he may be rewarded by never having to follow another. As everyone has observed, sleep taken before one is tired is the most restful and efficient. Upon this principle the last tip is based. Get rested before trying to sleep.

Years ago I helped with a patient whose physician had ordered that she get into bed upon reaching home after her day's work, be served dinner in bed, write letters or knit or chat with the members of her household until she fell asleep; but not arise until after seven in the morning. This routine was followed for several weeks with excellent results to her blood pressure, which had been very high when she had gone to the physician for help. With the new emphasis on counteracting tension in medicine, physicians are saying that muscle fatigue, or tiredness with all its consequences can only be treated with rest. Initially, for them, minimum rest consists of twelve continous hours in bed daily. The time may be spent reading, sleeping, watching television, or in any way; but must be in BED. If additional rest is necessary, the patient must stop work. If this is not sufficient, more time must be spent in bed. Occasionally this may be done at home; usually hospitalization is necessary if the entire hospital staff can be impressed that the patient would not be hospitalized except for the need for intensive rest, not to be awakened at 6:00 a.m. for temperature to be taken and the teeth to be brushed, etc.

In order to get rested without such a drastic routine, provided you are reading this book for personal help, you might get into bed an hour or more before your regular time for retiring. Don't spend so much time fussing around, on fol-di-rol and gadgetry and panaceas. Expect to sleep, and get the body rested. Do so night after night, and finally you will find yourself building up a reserve of rest and falling to sleep without the old struggle.

Didn't Benjamin Franklin say something about "Early to bed"? Didn't our own forefathers, who lived without electric lights, go to bed much earlier than we do? Don't peasants in less industrialized countries than ours, removed from the noise, rush, and glitter of big cities, seek repose at an early hour? If we wish to be saved from the pitfalls of extreme tension, which seems to be so annoying and disastrous in modern metropolitan society, should we not learn of Franklin, of our forebears, and of those in more simple cultures? They may have had their troubles and their diseases, but the chances are that they would not feel impelled to read a book on techniques in relaxation.

Index